BINSTED AND L_

Portrait of a Sussex Village

'Seclusion breathes everywhere'.

Edited by Emma Tristram

Compiled by the Binsted Book Group

Vicki Bryceson, Bob and Joy Davies, Sue and Tony Elphick, Penny Hadley,
John and Peggy North, Bill Pethers, Brendon Staker, David and Rosemary Tristram,
Emma and Mike Tristram, Luke and Michelle Wishart, Jo and Ron Withers, Celia Woodruff

Published by Friends of Binsted Church with the help of a grant from Awards for All

First published in 2002 by Friends of Binsted Church, Stable Cottage, Binsted, near Arundel, West Sussex, BN18 0LL.   Printed by St Richard's Press, Terminus Industrial Estate, Chichester, West Sussex.

ISBN: 0 9542920 0 6

Acknowledgements

The Binsted Book Group (Chairman, Bob Davies; Secretary, Sue Elphick; Treasurer, Tony Elphick) met regularly for nearly two years.   Our interviewers were Vicki Bryceson, Bob Davies, Sue Elphick, Bill Pethers and Emma Tristram.   Bill Pethers was our computer consultant.   The group hopes to continue to meet as the Binsted History Group.

Thanks are due to all who wrote contributions, gave interviews, donated documents, art works or photographs, wrote letters, telephoned or sent emails; and also to those who made contributions that were not used in the book.   All this information will form part of the archive of the Binsted History Group. Thanks also to P.Ll.Gwynn-Jones, Garter King of Arms, for giving permission for his letter of 1989 to be quoted, and to Patricia Balcazar and Richard Graham for allowing us to quote their tributes to Colin Baker.

We are also grateful to all those who have allowed photographs to be used.   Bill Pethers' collection of family photographs from the Read and Lewis families dates from about the 1860s to the early 20th century; Henry Lewis (born 1862), son of the Rector of Binsted, was a keen photographer, and many of them were taken by him.   Jean Hotston lent photographs taken by herself and Fred Hotston in the 1940s and 50s, including the Binsted signpost.   Rob Tutt lent photographs by Rodney Symes of his father, Reg, and John North.   Clare Druce, Sue Elphick, John North and Luke Wishart also lent photographs.

The painting reproduced on the cover is by Jenni Cassel – many thanks to her for allowing us to use it. The aerial photograph with labels was created using part of a photograph donated by Roger Smith of Gosport.   The Staker family tree was recreated on computer by Bill Pethers from an original in the possession of Brendon Staker, based on research by Muriel Haynes.   The painting of Binsted House in the 1940s by Ralph Ellis is owned by Mike and Emma Tristram.

Threshing at Binsted Park in the mid-1800s.

Contents

Introduction: Binsted and beyond

Emma Tristram

An ordinary place?

For many hundreds of years Binsted, near Arundel in West Sussex, was quite an ordinary place. In some ways it still is. There are thousands of other small villages or parishes in England composed of the same elements; scattered houses, woods, fields, trees, streams, valley, church. To Binsted's inhabitants, the way these elements are put together here has a unique charm, but inhabitants of other parishes might feel the same about their home patch. Binsted would not be 'worth the detour' in a tourist guide; it does not provide breathtaking panoramas or extreme walking experiences.

What has made it less ordinary is partly what has happened to the once very similar areas round about it. The plantation woodlands to the north and east, and worked-out gravel and sand pits to the north-east, are newer landscapes. Further east, the northern part of Tortington, once a wooded hill, is now a large suburb of Arundel. To the south and south-west, villages once small have grown large – Yapton and Barnham. To the west is another village, Walberton, which has also grown, though it has kept its character – perhaps because it has filled in between two older 'ends', rather than sprawling. Further south, a massive conurbation covers most of the coast, with a small gap at Climping.

In this sea of change, Binsted is now a small island of the past. Unlike many of the surrounding areas, the landscape of Binsted has retained its broad-leaved woodland and its historic pattern of houses, fields and woods, which has lasted over a thousand years. It never moved its farmhouses into an expanding village centre, as happened at Walberton in the 18th and 19th centuries. Looking further back, the small fields almost wholly enclosed in woodland recall the clearings which formed the first human settlements in this and other wooded areas, including the Downs.

By not doing what places round it have done, Binsted has acquired a new preciousness as a refuge – for people and wildlife. Walking here gives the mind a rest from the pace and demands of modern life, and many people do walk here, from Arundel and the surrounding villages. You can look back through the landscape at a way of life (very harsh in some ways) in which the land was people's job, their home and their life, everyone knew everyone else, and there was a much greater unity between people and their environment than there is now.

Pressure for change

The pressures (for more lucrative use of land, more houses, more roads, more development) which have changed the look of the areas around Binsted are also always at work trying to change Binsted itself. One of the articles in this book tells of our

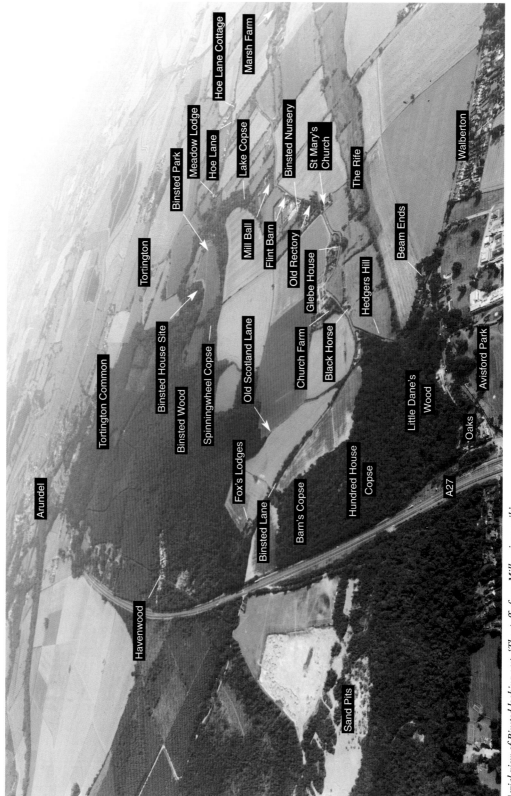

Hoe Lane Cottage

Marsh Farm

Meadow Lodge

Hoe Lane

Lake Copse

Binsted Nursery

St Mary's Church

Binsted Park

The Rife

Walberton

Tortington

Mill Ball

Flint Barn

Old Rectory

Glebe House

Beam Ends

Hedgers Hill

Tortington Common

Binsted House Site

Spinningwheel Copse

Old Scotland Lane

Church Farm

Black Horse

Binsted Wood

Little Dane's Wood

Avisford Park

Fox's Lodges

Oaks

Arundel

Binsted Lane

Barn's Copse

Hundred House Copse

A27

Havenwood

Sand Pits

Aerial view of Binsted looking east. 'The stuff of our Millennium quilt'.

The Shaw and Spinningwheel Copse, part of Binsted Woods. On winter evenings rooks pour along the tops of these trees. The so-called 'Green routes' suggested for the Arundel Bypass (being researched again, June 2002) would mean the Bypass emerged from the woods at this point. Painting by Felicity Fisher.

struggle to keep the Arundel Bypass out of Binsted in the 1980s and 90s. We succeeded – another route was chosen; but it was not built.

Of course, there is a new threat (2002): curiously, it is contained in the plan to make a South Downs National Park, in itself an attempt to save at least some areas from the same pressures. The proposed boundary for the Park cuts Binsted in two, including most of the woods and excluding all the rest. This leaves the rest of Binsted vulnerable, and may bring with it another attempt to put the Bypass through Binsted, south of the main block of woods.

At least Binsted is now acknowledged to be beautiful: the landscape consultants who advised the Countryside Agency about the new National Park said this area (Binsted and Tortington) was 'an attractive landscape which connects the wooded chalk downs to the Arun floodplain, and forms part of the setting to Arundel'. They saw the whole area as worthy of inclusion. (Mysteriously, the Countryside Agency has so far decided to ignore its advisers.)

It is no good waiting for a final chapter in the story of the defence of Binsted before publishing this book. Binsted will always be under threat because of its position on the crowded West Sussex coastal plain. Even if it is not split into two fragments of ancient countryside on either side of a new dual carriageway, along which the freight of Europe roars, it may one day form a suburb of some megalopolis of the future. This book celebrates the way it is now and remembers how it has been in the past; perhaps our celebration will also help preserve it for a while longer.

What is in Binsted?

Those attempting to preserve Binsted's character have become used to describing its beauties for various planning authorities. To bring out how varied Binsted is for the latest set of planners we listed its attractions:

Binsted Woods. 250 acres of very varied broad-leaved woodland – the largest such woodland remaining on the coastal plain of West Sussex.

Narrow belts of woodland. These connect the main mass of the woods with the rest of the parish, tying the whole landscape together.

Hedges. For instance, the overgrown hedges along Binsted Lane West, near the A27, provide a green 'tunnel' which makes a lovely entrance to the parish, and opens out to good views southwards, sloping gently towards the sea. These hedges contain many old coppiced trees.

Small, ancient fields, wholly or mostly enclosed in woodland.

Larger, undulating fields in the centre of Binsted where common land used to be.

Small, remote 'watermeadows' in the south, that used to be flooded and provide summer pasture for the farmers of the parish.

The Binsted Rife valley. Though not deep, this steep-sided valley is quite a dramatic feature for an area on the coastal plain. It is thought a catastrophic 'event' during melting after the last Ice Age may have created it.

Historic buildings. Binsted's 12th-century church (small, whitewashed, with the remains of a mediaeval wall-painting and a fine Norman font) is looked after by the local community and kept open at all times. It is much valued by visitors for its peaceful atmosphere. The small graveyard, with wonderful views up and down the Binsted Rife valley, is managed for conservation, with parts mown at different times so that wild flowers can flower. The church is Grade II listed, as are Church Farmhouse, Glebe House, Marsh Farmhouse, the Thatched Cottage in Hoe Lane, Meadow Lodge, and Morley's Croft.

Small streams and ponds. There are many of these, including two new lakes in the south of the parish, recently created by the landowner. These and other ponds are much visited by birds, including visitors from the Wildfowl and Wetlands Trust at Arundel, such as Mandarin ducks.

Atmosphere. Binsted has a secluded atmosphere often commented upon. A newspaper article of 1937 said of it: 'Seclusion breathes everywhere. Rich hedgerows and silent woods are around you. This tree-entwined village has peace with its isolation' (see Chapter 2). The main mass of the woods protects the whole area from the noise and disruption of the A27. The 'secret', enclosed fields also have a hidden quality. In the Binsted Rife valley, you feel cut off from human habitations, as they are hidden by the lie of the land and hedges and trees, though it is within easy walking distance of many houses in Walberton. The layout of Binsted Lane, a horseshoe-shaped 'dead end' for cars, is essential in preserving the sense of enclosure. Binsted is not, at present, a rat-run to anywhere.

An ancient parish

The area felt to belong to Binsted coincides closely with the ancient parish boundary. The civil parish of Binsted is now part of Walberton parish (joined to it in 1985, after a spell being joined to Tortington from 1933), but for centuries Binsted was an independent parish, raising its own taxes to look after its poor. It still has its own Parochial Church Council.

The old parish boundary on the western side is the stream at the bottom of the Rife valley. (Rife is a local word for a stream.) To the south and east, more watercourses

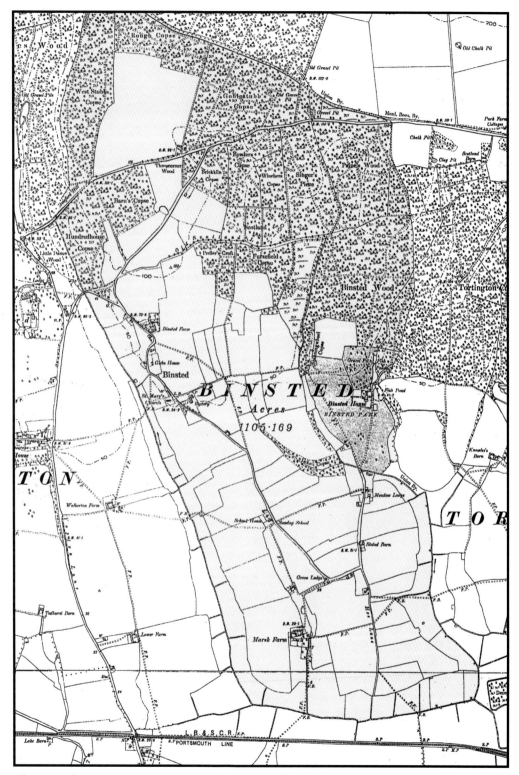

The 1880 Ordnance Survey map of Binsted parish (surveyed 1875). South of what is now the A27, and within the eastern parish boundary, Binsted's precious broad-leaved woodland still survives, much as in this map – although more has grown to the south. Outside this area, broad-leaved woodland has become plantations, usually conifers.

mark the parish boundary, all draining into the river Arun. Binsted Woods, in the northern part of the parish, are felt to be part of Binsted. Within the woods, the eastern parish boundary is well marked by an earth bank, and a change from broad-leaved woodland (in Binsted) to conifer plantations (on Tortington Common).

Bluebells in Spinningwheel Copse.

A chunk of the northern part of the parish was cut off when the A27 was dualled in the 1970s, and this now has rather a different character (old gravel pits and plantation woodland); in former years, it used to be where courting couples walked, being out of the way of the houses in the village. Also within the parish is the mobile home park of Havenwood, like a small, separate village hidden in the woods near the A27.

Wildlife

Binsted Woods are designated a Site of Nature Conservation Importance (this includes Little Dane's Wood, Hundred House Copse and Barn's Copse to the west, and the woodland belts to the south). Bluebell walks in woodland, along with drifts of early purple orchids and wood anemones, are an experience parents bring their children to Binsted to enjoy, using the many footpaths through the woods. But equally important are the less visible ferns, mosses, liverworts, sedges, lichens and fungi. The woods have a high score of Ancient Woodland Indicator Species.

Early morning walkers can see deer come out from the woods into the fields and across to the Rife valley. There are bats, badgers, foxes, and rabbits, also dormice and squirrels; and a wealth of birds – woodpeckers, owls and other raptors, tits, nightjars, woodcocks. The woods are also host to a multitude of insects such as Purple Emperor, White Admiral and Fritillary butterflies, moths, beetles and spiders. The best part of the woods for wildlife is the south-western part, especially the woodland edge, with its small enclosed fields and projecting belts and copses.

Binsted Woods have been much surveyed, and their value realised, in the course of researching the least damaging place to put a new Arundel Bypass. One report called them 'nationally important' (1992). Such a wealth of wildlife cannot be developed with conifers or other new planting, even within hundreds of years. Britain now has less than 2 per cent ancient woodland cover, and this decreases yearly. Three-quarters of what is left is in woods of 50 acres or less, so Binsted's 250 acres are extremely precious.

History

The fossils that can be found in Binsted recall the remote prehistory of the whole landscape, back to a period when it was all under the sea, including the Downs, and the chalk and flints were laid down at the bottom of the sea. Stone tools have been found in Binsted and worked flints can often be picked up from the paths, thrown up by farming. Two 'raised beaches', now buried underground, run through the parish in an east-west direction, one north and one south of the A27; they date back about half a million years to the time of Boxgrove Man, whose remains were found at nearby Eartham on the Downs, associated with one of the old beach lines.

A prehistoric earthwork (ditch and bank) runs north-south through Binsted, and north of the A27 as far as Madehurst on the Downs. It is probably part of the 'Chichester entrenchments', an enigmatic system of Iron Age fortifications centred on Chichester; there are few such systems in the country. These systems, now known as 'territorial oppida', may have been for defence, or to mark possession of a territory. The earthwork is visible in the fields north and south of Binsted church, and also in Hundred House Copse. Parts are designated an Ancient Monument. North of Binsted church, a 'bell pit', where a bell was cast, has been excavated by archaeologists. This was originally dug in the soft material which had partly filled the ditch of the historic earthwork.

In mediaeval times Binsted was famous for its pottery. 'Binsted ware' is found all along the coast, fairly rough and crude, but sometimes with a lively appliquéd 'face'. The best-known pottery works was in Hundred House Copse, near Hedgers Hill, and was excavated in the 1960s. It mainly made roof tiles. Recently (2000 and 2001) new excavations have suggested there was another pottery works the other side of Binsted Lane West, in the field opposite the pub. The pottery works depended on clay deposits – in fact on the nature of Binsted's subsoil, which contains sand, gravel, clay (Reading Beds) and flints. The name 'Brick Kiln Piece' for woodland near the A27 suggests bricks were also made. There are several pits in the woods where clay may have been dug out.

Binsted now

In social terms Binsted has changed very much in the last fifty years. In 1948, when Arthur Wickstead first lived at the Pub, he remembers that 'darts were all the go, and there were enough farm workers on Wishart's farm [including land outside Binsted] to make two teams of eleven players'. Now far fewer of the village's inhabitants work on the land, though a small part of the parish, Binsted Nursery, provides employment for many, though mostly from outside the parish, with intensive production of garden plants.

The advent of the car, the telephone and the computer brought professionals into what were once farm cottages or farm buildings: art, writing, architecture, music, photography, health, insurance, law, antiques, and house conversion are all fields in which recent inhabitants have laboured. Some people who work in the arts turn to work on the nursery, or the larger one at Walberton, when creativity does not pay. A few people still work on the farm, and there are rural businesses such as Bee Bee Kennels, and farm vehicle hire. The Elizabethan farmhouse at Marsh Farm is now an alternative healing centre which runs courses for practitioners.

When houses in Binsted are sold they can now fetch fabulous sums. The 'countryside', which used to be a home, job and way of life for people who lived here, is too often reduced now to a pretty view outside the window. How in these circumstances we stay together as a village, and retain our identity, is something to be discovered from this book.

Making the book

We have concentrated on what we can discover of the history of Binsted's people. The book is arranged chronologically, starting with a historical article based round the church. 'People from the past' (Chapter 2) highlights some of the individuals who can be glimpsed in the many fascinating historical documents we uncovered. To investigate more recent times, we turned to the memories of our long-standing inhabitants. We have tried to include mainly new material, rather than recycle what is already available.

When does gossip become history? Some of our interviewees tended to remember people by their looks (fat, red-faced, long-necked, 'painted like a Dutch doll'), their ailments and drink problems, or their extra-marital affairs and illegitimate children ('She was the one who was unfaithful!' 'The little girl in the churchyard – no-one knows who she belongs to.') The bland tone of so much local history suddenly became explicable.

Luckily there was plenty we could say. Life at the end of the 19th century is far enough away for gossip to have faded into history, yet near enough to have been passed on in memories and photographs. The Second World War produced a flood of memories: Clare Druce remembers with the intensity of a child's vision the details of everyday life, and how Binsted could be 'the best place on earth' even in a time of national emergency (Chapter 3). In Chapter 4 we have memories of the Pub and his family from Bill Pethers, and other insights about Binsted just after the war; and in Chapter 5 a collection of information about wartime and post-war air crashes in and near Binsted. Chapter 6, 'Recent memories', contains (among other things) two personal accounts of living in Binsted from Shelagh Archer and Jane Hollowood. Chapters 7 and 8 describe the Nursery, Friends of Binsted Church and the road campaign, and Chapter 9 looks at some of Binsted's legends.

Layout

We have used italics for personal, written statements, usually short. Roman type has been kept for extracts from interviews (and phone conversations and emails), and also for longer chapters written by one contributor (the exception is Chapter 3, a longer personal memoir, printed in italics). In chapters which are compilations, without an author's name, the linking passages are editorial. I hope these decisions help break up the text, but not too much, and give some idea of the range of different contributions, some written, some spoken.

Binsted and beyond

Why 'Binsted and beyond'? Because in the course of creating the book, we discovered that the more you find, the more there is to find. This book is only the tip of the iceberg of documents and interviews which we collected. Everything will be kept, so that the archive can be consulted by anyone who is interested. The Bibliography gives more information on local history resources.

Seeing Binsted in a wider context makes it seem like a connection in a spider's web of infinite extent. (Or, as John Heathcote put it, part of an infinite jigsaw.) Various articles take us not just to nearby villages, but to Victoria station in wartime, America and Africa. There is also, of course, our reputation for ghosts, though I like to think of Binsted as haunted simply by the rich past we have uncovered.

Chapter 1 Binsted church: a social history

Celia Woodruff

It is not known for how long a Christian place of worship has stood on the site where the little church of St. Mary now stands in Binsted. At the time of the great Domesday survey in 1086, no mention was made of a church in Binsted. We are told that the land was held by a man called Oismelin who was a tenant of Roger de Montgomery. Earl Roger was one of King William's 'right-hand men' and had been granted permission to build a castle at Arundel by the Conqueror in approximately 1086. Thus Binsted's association with Arundel has been close for at least 900 years.

As Arundel and other towns and communities developed, churches, priories and abbeys appeared in the locality, generally under the patronage of one or other of the great noblemen who had taken control of England after the Conquest of 1066. Binsted's foundation is unknown, but it may have been built by the monks of Tortington Priory, approximately 3 miles south-east of Binsted. However, no surviving evidence has been found to confirm such a connection. Tortington, dedicated to St Mary Magdalene, was a cell of the Augustinian Priory of Seez in Normandy. Augustinian houses were entirely independent of each other and not subject to superior control. Their estates were less extensive than those of other orders and their sympathies and relationships more local. The decades between 1110 and 1160 saw the greatest number of foundations. Tortington may have been founded by a member of the powerful De Albini family, one Lady Hadvisia Corbet. The old English name of Avis, as in nearby Avisford, is thought to be a shortened form of her name, and a small church such as Binsted could have been

Binsted church in 1995.

built by the monks to serve tenants on her estate.

What evidence there is strongly supports the likelihood that the little church was built about 1150, at approximately the same time as the priory church at Tortington. Tortington Priory is thought to have been founded before the reign of King John, which started in 1199. Binsted and Tortington church are similar in appearance and style, and 3 small windows of Norman origin in the chancel at Binsted date to approximately the mid twelfth century. The font, which is carved and has blind arcades, is also in the early Norman style and thought to be original to the church.

Early history

Whatever the actual date of its foundation, Binsted church would have served its village community then just as it does today. Religious adherence was very much more part of everyday life in Medieval England, and the church would have been one of the largest, if not the largest, stone building in the locality. It is largely unaltered from its original appearance. It has a cellular linear plan and although there is no division internally, it can be seen from the roofline that there is a break which separates the nave and chancel. At some point after it was built the division inside would have been evident from the rood beam, remnants of which are left on the north and south walls. Its date is unknown, but mouldings suggest that it is 14th century. On the north wall of the exterior is a buttress, now with a memorial stone set within it, which could have been the site of an external stair

St Margaret or St Mary (or St Ambrose? See Chapter 2). The surviving wall painting in Binsted church as it is now.

to the rood loft, needed to gain access to the statues on the beam within. We know from a later will that candles were placed by the rood. The rood beam carried a large cross, the rood, which would have been flanked by statues of the Virgin and St. John, providing worshippers with a striking reminder of the crucifixion scene. In a world where the majority of the population were unable to read or write, it was visual imagery which enabled people to learn about their faith.

As well as the remains of the rood beam, Binsted has remnants of a set of wall paintings, which would have provided powerful images of the Gospel and other religious teachings. Like the rood, these images are largely destroyed, through the passage of time and possibly through deliberate destruction, but a mystery rests within the original north chancel window, where a painting of a female crowned figure and of a representation of what appears to be a three-branched tree can be seen. For many years the figure was thought to be the only known representation of St Margaret of Scotland. The writing above the figure, which is now gone, was recorded in 1888 as 'S/A MARG:' this has been interpreted as a shortening of the Latin form of St Margaret, but recently

BINSTED CHURCH:
Window on N. of Chancel.

The surviving wall painting in Binsted church as recorded by P.M.Johnston in 1888.

consideration has been given to the possibility that it could be 'St Mary'.

The painting was at first thought to be coeval to the foundation of the church, but it may be later. The lady appears to be crowned and this adds credence to the claim that the figure represents St. Margaret of Scotland. However, since St Margaret was not canonised until 1250 she is an unlikely subject if the painting is as early as the church. Possibly the dedication is to St Mary Magdalene, as it is at Tortington, but the crowned figure is more likely to be a depiction of the Virgin, as queen of Heaven. This would have been appropriate to the time, as a renewal of religious fervour re-awakened a popular appeal to the cult of the Virgin and saints. The three-branched tree might represent the Trinity and this would suit a depiction of the Virgin. The theme of the coronation of the Virgin seems to have developed in the 12th Century and this would therefore be appropriate to the little church at Binsted.

Another, more intriguing hypothesis is that the figure is of St Margaret of Antioch. This saint is usually shown with a dragon at her feet and a cross in her hand. She was honoured as the patron saint of women in childbirth, and images of her may have been 'thank offerings' for a safe confinement. Was it the Lady Hadvisia who endowed Binsted and commissioned the painting in the chancel of the church? Not only was she herself married, but she had also been the concubine of Henry I, bearing a son, Reginald, who became Earl of Cornwall in the reign of King Stephen (1135-1154). The mystery remains, and speculation should not cloud our judgement, but in the absence of real evidence, all these possibilities may be considered.

While the origins of the church are unknown, there is no doubt that Tortington Priory was connected with Binsted from 1291 onwards. The priory had 'appropriated' the rectory at this time, and these links probably remained until the Dissolution of the monasteries in the 1530s. Appropriation had become common in the 13th and early 14th century and was frequently a means of boosting monastic revenues. It allowed the monks of the priory to claim the income and tithes of the parish. In return they were responsible for the provision and support of a vicar for the parish. A document which gives details of the value of the tithes and income at Binsted 'in the 15th year of the reign of Edward III' (1342) tells of the rectory of the church having lands and tenements which 'are worth yearly 20 marks' with the vicarage valued at 10 marks. It also notes that the vicar of the same parish had glebe land amounting to 10 acres worth 25 marks, and other meadows and pasture worth 10 marks. Tithes of, amongst other things hay, cider, hemp, pigs, foals, lactage, honey and eggs added up to a further 16 marks annually. Mortuary oblations, offerings to the church at the time of a death, and 'other small tithes arising at the altar' added an additional 20 marks. It noted that there were no other benefices in the parish and that there were only farmers. It can be assumed that the benefice of Binsted at that time brought a healthy income to the priory at Tortington, but it would seem that the incumbent vicar also enjoyed a reasonable living.

The horrors of the Black Death

Such prosperity was severely reduced when the nation was struck by the fearsome bubonic plague or Black Death. It struck England in the autumn of 1348 and decimated a large cross-section of the population, spreading from the south coast throughout most of the British Isles. Approximately one third of the population was wiped out. None were spared and both monastic and lay communities suffered great losses in town and country. No records exist to gauge the effect the 'pestilence' or 'great mortality', as it was known, had on either Binsted or indeed on the priory at Tortington, but it is safe to assume that both communities would have been seriously affected by the plague. Along the coast in Seaford it was reported in 1356 that 'it was so desolated by plague and the chances of war that men living there are so few and so poor that they cannot pay their taxes or defend the town'.

The implications for the inhabitants of Binsted can only be guessed, but since the church was closely associated with Tortington by this time, the likelihood is that there were times when the villagers had no priest because of the high mortality rate of the religious communities. Similarly land rents and labour shortages in post-plague times were such that landowners experienced falling income and higher labour charges, an effect which Tortington would almost certainly have suffered like so many other religious houses. In 1414, the vicarage of Binsted was exempted from taxes, showing a marked contrast in its prosperity from the assessment made in 1342, just 7 years before the onset of the plague. In 1424 it was stated that the poverty of the living had led to the neglect of services, but a vicar was resident in the village in 1440.

A preoccupation with death and the after-life had followed the disaster of the Black Death, and obits or memorial masses were considered essential for the salvation of the soul for those who could afford to pay the priest to say them. Similarly, alms-giving was considered a powerful and effective way of salvation for the departed. Binsted folk must have been as susceptible to the fears of hell and damnation as other communities. Even as late as 1534 one such instruction was given by a John Sharpe, who, in his will, requested that an obit be said yearly at Binsted for his soul and for the souls of his father, mother, his brother Sir Robert, his friends and all other Christian souls. He further instructed his executors to give out bread, ale and cheese to the poor people at the time when the obit was said. Thirteen years later in 1547 the vicar of the parish, William Fotherlye, willed that a memorial mass be said for his soul, and that all people of his parish should receive a gift of money, bequeathing half as much to the children as to the adult souls in his care.

Worship, too, had developed from the simple celebration of the sharing of bread and wine of the early centuries of Christianity to a highly charged and elaborate ceremony in Medieval England. It is unlikely that there were pews in the nave of the church at this time. Indeed, the only form of seating would have been around the walls of the church, creating our expression 'the weakest go to the wall'. Pews were probably added sometime in the 15th century as the importance of preaching as well as the Mass was introduced. The rood screen, which seems to date from the early 14th century, would have separated the church into nave and chancel. The screen at Binsted would have provided a sort of window on the proceedings in the chancel. Rood screens were usually solid only up to waist height, with the upper section carved into ornate windows through which the congregation could see. Parishioners would have been aware of the gospel stories from the wall paintings which have now almost disappeared. The ordinary people seldom received Communion, but were witness to the priest celebrating High Mass at the altar at the east end of the church. We can perhaps imagine this as a sort of theatre where ritual and mystery were to be seen in the act of worship before them. This could well have been the only opportunity the poor had to experience such colour and drama, and may have been a high point in a weekly round of drudgery and hard work.

Binsted, the Reformation and the dissolution of the monasteries

All this was to change in the fifteenth and sixteenth centuries. The Reformation, which in England had its roots in Lollardy, was led by an intellectual, John Wycliffe. His was the first complete translation of the Bible into English in 1396, and he also inspired a move towards greater emphasis on Holy Scripture. Although printed Bibles were not widely available for another century, by 1538 clergy were instructed to have an English Bible available in every parish church. By no means every parish conformed to this order, either because the parish could not afford one or because the vicar was opposed to it. Where, one wonders, is the one which Binsted had, if indeed it had one at all? Wycliffe also poured scorn on the wealth of the church and the unworthiness of some of the clergy. Evidence of such unworthiness can be found at Tortington, where in 1376 the prior, John Palmere, was found to be 'careless not only of property, but also of his own good fame'. It was stated that he was living dissolutely outside the monastery and should be put on trial for such behaviour. Since Tortington was responsible for the provision of a vicar at Binsted, we can only speculate as to the care or 'cure' (from which our word curate comes) of souls which was provided for Binsted at the time.

Lollardy did not, in the end, cause any major upheavals in church practice in England, but later attacks on the practices of the Catholic church in continental Europe by Erasmus and his Lutheran church were to cause irreversible changes to church and community life. These changes did not reach England until the early 1500s, and were prompted to a great extent by anti-clericalism. But it was the marital problems of Henry VIII which finally triggered the English Reformation. It was to transform the Catholic Church in England into the Protestant Church of England of which Binsted is part. Henry broke with Rome and the Pope because the Pope refused to grant an annulment of the King's marriage to Catherine of Aragon. In a series of manoeuvres Henry passed Acts of Parliament which stripped the Catholic Church hierarchy of its legislative powers in England.

The first Act of Supremacy of 1534 made Henry head of the church in England and enabled him to take control of both material and doctrinal property which had hitherto belonged to the monastic communities and to the Pope. The Dissolution of the monasteries followed, as Henry took under his control all land and property which had

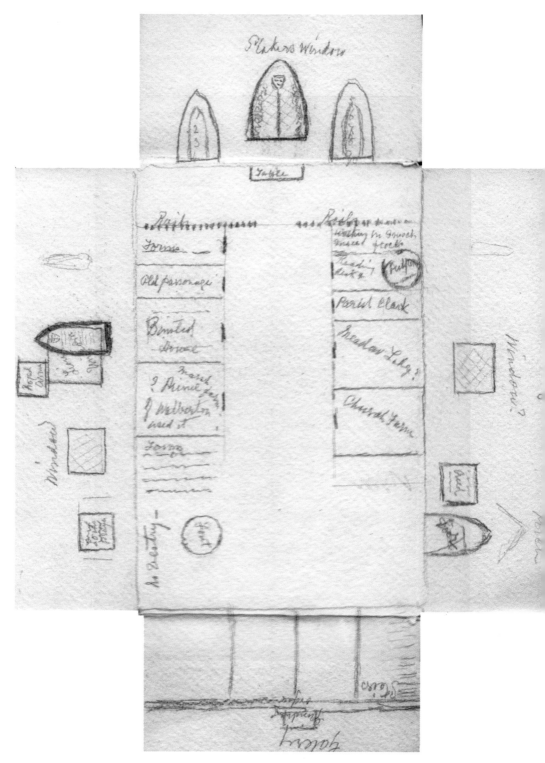

Sketch by Charlotte Read showing the Georgian interior of Binsted church before the 'restoration' of 1867-8. This was made on card so the 'walls' could stand upright.

previously been owned by the church.   In order to justify such an act, Henry 'cashed in' on the unrest and suspicions which had been raised by the Lollards and by the Lutherans of the Reformation movement and sent crown servants on visitations to inspect the state of monastic institutions and property.   Binsted, as a vicarage of the Priory of Tortington, would have been subject to this valuation. A certificate for the County of Sussex gives details of Tortington Priory's state in 1536.   The house, it declared, was wholly in ruin.   The surrender of Tortington would have happened between 1536 and 1540, and while the exact date is unknown, the effect for Binsted was that the right to appoint a vicar thereafter fell to the Crown.

With its new-found powers after the Dissolution, the state also used the church as a means of imposing new styles of worship and law and order on its citizens.   The clergy were required to keep parish registers from 1538.   They were to record baptisms, marriage and burials in each community.   If records were kept at Binsted there is no trace of them at this early stage.   Binsted's surviving registers begin in 1638 and make interesting reading!   Binsted, as elsewhere, would also have seen the introduction of Cranmer's Prayer Book in 1549.   This was a measure introduced in the reign of Edward VI and its novelty was that it was in English.   For the first time, parishioners could understand the progress of the service in their mother tongue, instead of the Latin which had been used before.

For the brief period of Queen Mary I, who was a staunch Catholic, the nation reverted to papal authority.   However, when Elizabeth I succeeded in 1558 the congregation would have begun to experience what we are now more familiar with as the Church of England.   In 1559 the Act of Uniformity imposed compulsory attendance at church on Sundays and holy days, with a fine of 12d for those who ignored it.   The churches were used to spread news regarding any statutes or doctrine which the state chose to impose, a concept which simply had not existed in pre-Dissolution days.   Also in 1559, the second Act of Supremacy was passed, making Elizabeth the Supreme Governor of the Church of England.

A move away from strong Catholic traditions caused the destruction of so-called 'papist' images and idolatry.   Scorn was thrown upon such superstitious practices as the obits and mortuary oblations of an earlier period and the change in attitude was largely responsible for the disappearance of traditions and works of art of the mediaeval church. Sometime in the second half of the century, Binsted probably lost the wall paintings and the rood screen which had been an integral part of the celebration of the medieval mass. The rood screen was removed, the wall paintings whitewashed.   In place of the wall paintings orders were given that the Royal Arms of England be displayed in all parish churches, and that the Lord's Prayer, the Ten Commandments and the Creed be painted on boards and prominently displayed in the church.

There is no evidence left in the church itself of these so called 'black letter texts' at Binsted, but notes on a sketch of the church remembered as it was before the 1868 restoration suggest it had them.   The sketch, by Miss Charlotte Read of Binsted House, shows two tablets with commandments placed either side of the altar.   A second board on the south wall close to the south door is annotated 'creed' and a third board on the north wall close to the font described as 'Lord's Prayer'.   Also on the north wall is a board described as 'Lion and Unicorn', perhaps the Royal Arms of England?   If these texts were in the church, it is quite probable that they were placed there soon after 1560, when the decree was published.

A second English Prayer Book was also introduced, which gave a broader interpretation of the meaning of the sacrament of Holy Communion. Instructions were given for the wearing of vestments which retained the style of the mediaeval mass. The more Puritan elements of the Protestant reformers bitterly objected to this. In 1567 there appears to have been such a dispute between the vicar, Robert Knight, and churchwardens. As with much of what happened to Binsted's church life in the next four centuries, such changes probably depended on the inclinations of the incumbents who held the living at the time of the imposition of these Acts of Parliament.

The absence or presence of a priest would, of course, have had a major impact on the religious life of the parish. In Binsted another effect of the Dissolution was the change of control of the benefice which became the property of the Crown. Until 1575 vicars were presented by the Crown. It seems however that the advowson, the right of presentation of the vicar, was sold after that as in 1605 it was the property of a Jane Shelley. This was a means of raising revenue, and many advowsons were sold by the Crown for this reason after 1536. The right of presentation was again sold in 1615 to Sir Garrette Kempe of Slindon, together with Binsted Manor, and remained in the same family until 1863. This effectively cut off the long association which Binsted and Tortington had shared since at least 1291.

From the mid-16th to the mid-19th century the practice of pluralism among the clergy was not uncommon. By 1820 a survey showed that 60% of benefices were held in plurality. Pluralism was the ownership of more than one benefice by the same rector or vicar. Binsted experienced its fair share of such practices, and was not well served by some of its clergy during this time. This may not have been the fault of the rector or vicar, who may well have had to survive on a small stipend paid by a lay rector, or on a rectorial income which had been stripped of much of its wealth by earlier transactions after the Dissolution. Several incumbents were associated with neighbouring parishes, such as Francis Heape who was initially resident in 1605, but who had let his glebe house by 1615. His ministry did not cease, however, until 1634. Another vicar, William Turner, also held the benefice of Walberton from 1696 to 1701, and lived at Walberton, thus forming a link which was to be repeated in the 20th century. From 1701 to 1863 the incumbent of Slindon also held the benefice of Binsted, but lived at Slindon. In the absence of the vicar, curates were sometimes appointed and this was the case in 1662, 1758, 1769 and 1844. Church attendance at the time was compulsory, but according to a religious census taken in 1676 there were only 21 families attending church at the time.

Regular weekly services may not have been the order of the day, and in some years it was noted that the vicar had preached only once during the year. On other occasions the residents of Binsted were recorded as having gone to hear preachers at Walberton. Whatever the number of sermons was, it is likely that they were deemed to be of major doctrinal importance in the 1600s. From the evidence of the sketch of the church as it was before 1868, it seems Binsted had a 'triple-deck' pulpit which was probably installed sometime in the 17th century, only to be removed in the 19th century. These large pulpits were intended to dominate the church, rendering the altar and chancel of less importance in church ministry. The teaching of Scripture and the importance of the Bible were better emphasised by the prominence given to these pulpits and demonstrated the shift away from the sacramental practices of the Catholic Church.

In 1662 another version of the Prayer Book was ordained, and has survived to this day as the much-loved Book of Common Prayer. It is still used alongside more modern styles of services at Binsted. These changes went on against a backdrop of turbulent change in England. Residents of Binsted would have lived through the death of Elizabeth in 1603 and the drama of the Stuart monarchies of James I and Charles I which ended in Charles's beheading in 1649. Civil war also raged between 1640 and 1650. After a period of governance under Cromwell, the monarchy was restored in 1660 when Charles II returned from exile in France. More was to come, with controversy over the Catholic inclinations of Charles II's successor, James II. In 1688, the throne was handed to James's daughter Mary and her Dutch consort, William. They ruled into the early 18th century. Binsted's population would almost certainly have been affected by these events, despite the smallness of the community. Perhaps some went off to join in the civil war, but on which side we are unlikely ever to know. Others would have been affected by the hardship and poverty caused by bad harvests such as those of 1659, 1660 and 1661. For those who remained at home, the parish church would have been one of the main sources of news from the outside world and the only source of help when disaster struck.

Georgian and Regency church life

The care of the poor and the infirm had traditionally been the role of the monasteries. At the Dissolution the hospitality of the monasteries disappeared almost at a stroke, leaving a void in the care of the destitute. Growing numbers of vagrants and poverty-stricken individuals were seen as a threat to law and order. The introduction of the office of Lord and Deputy Lieutenants of each county and the increased role of the Justice of the Peace in the local community was caused in part by the removal of the monastic role of care. The parish became the core of this system of local government and the activities of Binsted's more wealthy residents in law enforcement and poor relief had clearly become established by the beginning of the 18th century.

The records in the 'Poor Books' and vestry meetings from 1727 onwards give an insight into the way the Elizabethan Poor Relief Acts of 1598 and 1601 were being practised. These Acts laid down that each parish was responsible for the support of the poor living there. The poor were divided into the 'able-bodied' poor or 'sturdy beggars' and the impotent poor. The former were considered to be poor due to idleness and were undeserving of relief. If they did not belong to the parish they were returned to the parish of their birth or to the place where they had last lived for a year. Failing that they were placed in a house of correction which would employ and punish them. More compassionate care was given to the impotent poor, those who were in poverty through no fault of their own such as orphans and widows. The remedy for such persons was outdoor relief or shelter in the workhouse provided by the parish.

These measures were supervised and carried out by the Overseers of the Poor, often the churchwardens, who were responsible for administering poor relief and collecting the poor rate from local landowners to pay for any such relief. In Binsted a workhouse or poorhouse was built on the north side of the church although the date of its origin is unknown. The enforcement of these laws in Binsted is demonstrated in 1760, when Edward Staker was the Overseer. A certain Jane Leggat was the object of the relief, and

The Staker memorial tablet in Binsted church.

was provided with seercloth (waxed cloth). A year later the parish paid for the nursing of a Dame Coot and her subsequent burial expenses. She was clearly in very poor health by the time poor relief was given and must have been classified as impotent poor. A number of other parishioners' burial costs were also met out of poor relief at intervals.

Thankfully, not all poor relief went to the cost of burying the dead. Payments do, however, indicate the extent of the poverty experienced by the poor. In 1782 Edward Staker had become the churchwarden, while the task of Overseer had fallen to Ed Float and Richard Alcock. Payments at this time were made for two pairs of pattens (shoes) and for an apron, the use of which is not stated. Other payments went to the upkeep and maintenance of the poorhouse, such as the weekly pay of Dame Bassett, who was most probably the mistress of the poorhouse, and for the cost of candles, faggots (fuel for the fire) and a carriage.

Edward Staker died in 1825 and is commemorated in a wall plaque on the chancel nave at Binsted. It states that he was a Justice of the Peace, and thus played a prominent part in law enforcement in his locality. Along with his memorial is an extensive list of his relatives who were also buried in the church. The classical style of the plaque is typical of the artistic taste so popular at the time. The burial sites of the more humble members of the parish are not recorded with elaborate headstones or memorials but like the Stakers, most would have been laid to rest in the little churchyard close to where they had lived and worked.

Binsted's Victorian revival

Hardship would have been a part of everyday life for many of Binsted's population. Life in the early 19th century would have improved little if at all for most people. By the 1820s the old poor relief system was so inadequate that legislation was passed which was to see the end of the Overseers' duties in the parish. The Poor Law Amendment Act of 1834 transferred the responsibility of the care of the poor from the parish to a larger secular area called the Poor Law Union. Binsted was included in the Westhampnett Union, and the poorhouse next to the church was no longer used for the purpose of shelter for the local destitute. This effectively brought to an end the close ties which the church had in the care of the poor of the parish.

The living had been occupied throughout these changes by the Smelt family. From 1781 to 1854 the benefice was held by John Smelt and then by his son, Maurice. At the end of March 1851 a nation-wide religious census was ordered. Every parish was required to give a return of the numbers attending church at every service of the day. This was a response to the growing concern in Victorian England about the state of the Established Church at the time. In Binsted the rector reported that there were 170 seats in church. On the day of the census he noted that the weather was showery, and that 95 people attended worship. A church service was held at Binsted every Sunday alternately in the morning and evening. He also reported that the average attendance was 150.

At the time of the census, the church would have still had furnishings which we can speculate were added through the 17th and 18th centuries. In addition to the 'triple-deck' pulpit, the pews at the time seem to have included some box pews and others reserved for specific families of the village. There was also a gallery at the west end. The pews were possibly a relic of the custom of pew rents which had grown over the post-Reformation centuries. It reflected the close association between the church and the landed gentry of a local area, who were determined to retain their status within parish society. This included the reservation of specific pews, often small enclosed areas or 'boxes', which were reserved by means of a payment of rent to the church to preserve ownership. The sketch which remains of Binsted's pre-1868 appearance clearly shows the division of space between the local land-owning families and the labouring population. The Reverend Smelt's comment in the 1851 census that 124 of the 170 seats were 'free' gives a clue as to the number of pews which were subject to the 'pew rent'. The gallery may have been used for a small band of musicians, a relatively common form of musical accompaniment for an 18th-century congregation, a congregation which by today's standards would have been judged as large in so small a parish!

Church attendance did not seem to be a particular issue for the rector of Binsted at the time, but changes were to come to Binsted with the advent of a new rector in the second half of the 19th century. It seems that the new rector was one of a growing band of clergy who were determined to re-establish the importance of the Church of England in Victorian England. In 1863 the advowson was sold by the Slindon House estate to John Bones who presented his son, Henry Christopher Bones, who changed his name to Lewis in 1869. Henry Lewis was obviously intent on bringing religion back into the lives of his parishioners. The family re-established the rector as a resident of Binsted having built a substantial new rectory on glebe land opposite the church, this being completed by 1865.

The Reverend Henry Bones set to and drew up extensive restoration plans for the inside of the church. From photographs which have survived, it is clear that he replaced the old rood screen, lost at the Reformation, with what was considered a faithful replica of the original. The box pews were removed and pew benches which remain today were installed. The triple-deck pulpit was replaced by the less prominent version which is still in the church now. These changes suggest that Henry was a supporter of the High Church or Tractarian movement of the Victorian church. They were determined to revive the customs of a more Anglo-Catholic tradition, with an emphasis on the sacraments and the role and authority of the church. This was in contrast to alternative movements, the so-called 'Evangelicals' who emphasised the importance of Scripture, and the Broad Church movement who, with the burgeoning developments of the scientific professions and such men as Charles Darwin, were beginning to challenge the content of biblical and theological reasoning. These are simplistic explanations, but nevertheless, place Binsted at the heart of the growing religious debates of the time.

Binsted's rector did not stop at purely theological reform. He invested his not inconsiderable private means in the education and welfare of the children of Binsted, and supported the new National School at Walberton so that Binsted children could attend as well. Services at Binsted were increased in number and by 1884 communion was being held eight times a year, significantly more than had been available in the parish for some considerable time, perhaps even since pre-Reformation times. The Lewis family clearly made an impact on the lives of the people of Binsted, and the many photographic records which survive are testimony to the significance of Henry Lewis's efforts.

The twentieth century

After Henry's death in 1908 the living was occupied first by Alfred Harre and then by William Drury, whose incumbency ended in 1943. While less is known about these two rectors, they would have cared for a parish which would have been acutely aware of the fears and dangers of a nation at war. With its proximity to the coast, Binsted would have experienced these fears in the Great War, when some of its young men would have gone off to serve in the forces. By the time of the Second World War, the development of the Air Force as a significant fighting force brought even greater danger to the area. Memories of the air raids are vivid in the minds of Binsted residents at the time, and no doubt prayers were said for the safe return of airmen from the local airfields as well as for local people involved in the war effort. In the year 2000 a memorial was erected on the north wall of the church commemorating the loss of four Canadian airmen locally. These events only serve to emphasise the role of the little parish church in the ebb and flow of village life over the centuries.

Sketching Binsted church in the 1950s.

Since 1943 the rectory of Binsted has been joined with the vicarage of Walberton with the priest serving both communities. The advowson is now held by the Bishop of Chichester. Five incumbents have stamped their own particular style and theological leanings on the little church since 1943, and residents of the village have continued to serve the church in various ways. In 1947 the Victorian rood screen was removed. As in earlier centuries, baptisms, marriages and funerals still take place according to the needs of the parishioners.   In order to maintain the fabric of this ancient church, a charitable trust, the Friends of Binsted Church, holds an annual Strawberry Fair, thus bringing together churchgoers and non-churchgoers in a community effort prompted by parochial pride and affection.   This again is a reflection of earlier generations in Binsted when 'church ales' would probably have been held in the churchyard for the purpose of celebration and community gatherings.   The history of St Mary's, Binsted is a fascinating microcosm of the social and religious history of England over the last nine hundred years.   In local terms however it has been the focal point of much of what Binsted stands for today.   No doubt the little church will continue to offer a focal point for community life and Christian worship for many more centuries to come.

Information regarding the records of Binsted Church can be found at West Sussex Records Office.   The Sussex Archaeological Collections and the Sussex Record Society collections contain many interesting pieces of research about the church.   They too can be found at the Records Office and also at local libraries.   The Victoria County History of Sussex contains many of the primary source references made within the text.

Chapter 2   People from the past

St Ambrose   *Emma Tristram*

While sorting out the pictures for this book, I took another look at the lettering in the 1888 record of the mediaeval wall painting that still exists in Binsted church, though now much deteriorated and without its lettering.   (The lettering, already damaged in 1888, has been interpreted as St Margaret or more recently St Mary: see Chapter 1.)   I saw S A M, rather widely spaced, then some fragmentary letters.   The S could be short for Saint, rather than part of ST or S/A.   So the name of the saint might begin with AM.   I thought of Ambrose, and realised his name fitted the remains of the other letters and also filled the space, which other interpretations do not.

One feature of our saint is the strange-looking three-branched 'tree of life' on the opposite side of the window.   Looking up St Ambrose (c. 339-97 AD) in *The Saints in Christian Art*, I was very surprised to learn that the symbol most often found with him is a 'three-thonged scourge…the meaning of which has been very variously explained'. One explanation is that it refers to his severity against the Arians (heretics who did not accept that Jesus was divine).   'The three thongs are generally taken to symbolize the Holy Trinity.'   This is also what our 'tree of life' is taken to symbolize, with its three branches carefully plaited to emphasise both three-ness and one-ness.   It is possible that it is not only a tree of life but also a reference to St Ambrose's 'three-thonged scourge'.

Another puzzling aspect of our saint is her/his headdress, now mostly disappeared. It has been called a 'wimple', or seen as a crown.   St Ambrose is often shown wearing the clothes and mitre of a bishop.   The unexplained headdress could have been a form of mitre, decorated with jewels.   Its curved sides could be a halo.   The monks at Tortington were Augustinian monks, and St Ambrose helped convert St Augustine to Christianity.   The figure is pointing with one hand towards the altar, and St Ambrose wrote a treatise on the Sacraments.   He is often shown holding a book; our figure's other hand was recorded in 1888 as a curious oblong shape, but it could have been a hand holding a book.   Looking closely at what is left of the painting, I saw little parallel stripes in the right place which might have represented the pages of a closed book.   The present feminine curve of the body, and romantic trailing sleeves, are due to a loss of paint.   I think St Ambrose is definitely a name to add to the other possibilities.

The Staker family   *Brendon Staker*

In years gone by, the Staker family would have been a well-respected family and well-known also for their generosity to the poor people of local villages.   They would have been people of real estate, owning lands and houses in Binsted, Yapton, Climping, Ford, Tortington, Chichester, Westbourne, Aldingbourne, Southwater, Tillington and numerous other places.

Two local farms still run today with the name Stakers Farm.   One is in Yapton; owned by Benjamin Staker II (1785-1848), the farm was sold in 1837.   The house opposite Stakers

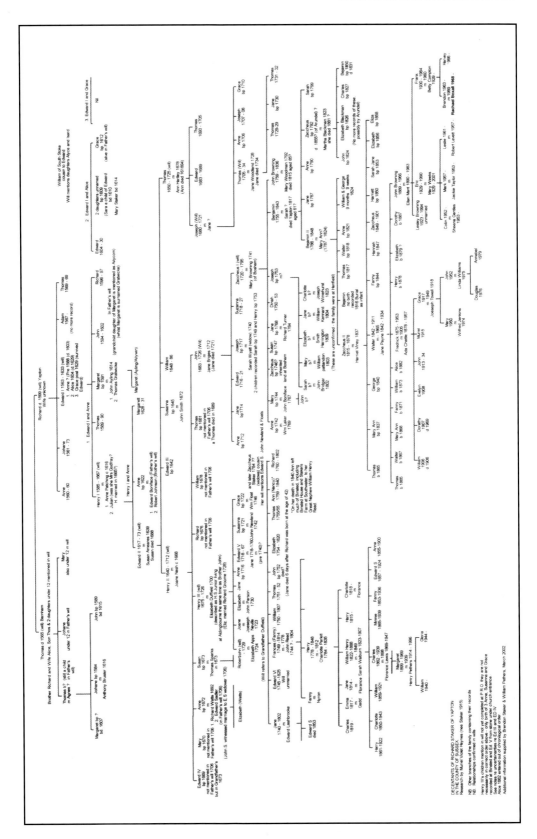

Farmhouse, now called Yew Tree Nursing Home, was built by Benjamin's father. Both houses resemble the old Binsted House in style. The other farm is at Stakers Lane, Southwater, near Horsham. I would not be surprised if Stakers had been living in the Binsted area for a thousand years, but obviously there are no records to prove this.

According to the Stakers' wills, Richard Staker of Yapton owned Binsted House in 1599. His eldest son Edward I (1563-1633) inherited it. It then passed to Henry I (1588-1667), then on to Edward II (1617-1673), then to Henry II (1640-1712), and on to Henry III (1675-1726). Henry III was the brother of John, my six-times-great-grandfather. From then on Binsted House was owned by distant cousins. Edward V (1718-1767) owned it, who was baptized at Binsted Church on 4 May 1718. The last male Staker to inherit Binsted House was Edward VI (1745-1825). Edward VI was a Justice of the Peace and did not marry. There were no sons to pass it on to, so it was passed on to his sister Ann (1757-1840), and the house was then inherited from her by the Read family.

The Staker family tree was compiled by my great-aunt, Muriel Haynes, who was born in Walberton. It took her over fifteen years to complete, and endless days in the West Sussex Records Office and Somerset House in London. W.S.R.O. holds many of my family's wills and that is how she compiled the early lines. She had great difficulty tracing where Richard Staker was buried. She came across a possible answer to the mystery in the will of his great-grandson, Edward Staker II (1617-1673), which said: 'My will and desire is that my executors hereafter named doe see my body decently buried in the churchyard of Yapton aforesaid under the stone where my great-grandfather layeth buried. And I desire that Edward Burnand minister of Yapton shall preach my funeral sermon to whom I give for his pains 20 shillings.'

Zaccheus Staker (1720-1795) married Mary Browning of Bosham in 1741, and the name Browning was then much used as a middle name for nearly 200 years. My uncle, who

Zaccheus Staker.

Harriet Viney.

Miss Fanny Read at the piano. Drawing by Edward Staker Read from a sketch book of 1875.

died in 1994, was named Lesley Browning Staker. Zaccheus was connected with Meadow Lodge, Binsted – he possibly lived there. The house was built by his son-in-law, William Laker, who married his daughter Anne in 1769. Zaccheus' son, also Zaccheus, inherited lands at Bosham from his mother.

The Staker arms

In 1989 Brendon Staker asked the College of Arms to investigate the armorial bearings depicted on the memorial in Binsted Church to Edward Staker of Binsted. The reply by P.Ll.Gwynn-Jones, then Lancaster Herald, was as follows:

I find that the Arms in question, without a Crest, were established in favour of one Anthony Stocker of Chilcompton in the County of Somerset in 1623. They may be blazoned as follows: Gyronny of six azure and argent three birds gules. Unfortunately, the birds are not specifically blazoned or described. However, they are almost certainly intended to be popinjays or parrots. The arms are a differenced version of the Arms of Sir William Stocker who was Lord Mayor in 1484. Sir William bore the gyronny of azure and argent with three green popinjays.

Anthony Stocker of Chilcompton was unable to prove his descent from the above mentioned Sir William Stocker; and the arms allowed to him were suitably differenced by rendering the popinjays gules (red).

In order for Edward Staker to have been entitled to the Arms displayed on his Memorial, it would have been necessary for him to have a legitimate male line descent from the above Anthony Stocker of Chilcompton. However, in my opinion the surname of Stocker is quite separate and distinct from that of Staker. Secondly, the Staker family of Binsted would not appear to have any connection with the Stockers of Dorset and Somerset.

He then traced the Staker line back from the Edward Staker of the memorial (Edward VI), baptized at Binsted in 1745, to Edward Staker II, baptized 1617 at Walberton, and concluded;

This tentative line of descent goes beyond the 1623 entry in Somerset. It suggests that the Staker family had been in the area of Binsted long before the Stockers of Somerset officially established their entitlement to Arms. It therefore seems a clear example of one family erroneously adopting the Arms of another family of similar surname but with whom there was no connection.

People in the 'Poor Books'

The name of Edward Staker appears very often, both as a landowner and as an Overseer, in the 'Poor Books', or account books of the Overseers of the Poor, described in the last chapter. These give us many glimpses of individuals in 18th-century Binsted. The two earliest books preserved in the West Sussex Records Office (Par 22/30/1 and 2) cover the years 1727 to 1831; from 1759 expenditure, as well as income, is shown.

The lists of yearly income from individual landowners could be used by someone with time on their hands to track the ownership of land and how much money it brought in. In a typical year, 1754, the main landowners were Richard Alcock (paid £7.17s.6d.), the Vicarage (paid £4.7s.6d.), William Float (paid £9.9s.0d.), and Edward Staker (paid £4.7s.6d.). 'The Lord's Mead' produced £2.7s.1/2d. But more immediately interesting are the payouts to the poor.

Sometimes a name or person is only mentioned once: in 1772 'Mary Hornsby, in want, 1s.'; the same year, 'paid 2 shillings for the travelling woman's child; for digging the grave, 2s.' In 1786, 'a pair of crutches for Ferdinand'. Sometimes the entries tell a story; in 1783 'Eliz. Croucher at her child's death for bread, 2s.; watching with Croucher's child, 2s.6d.; laying forth, 1s.6d.; paid for digging grave, 2s.; parish coffin for Croucher's child, 6s.6d.' (Was the travelling woman's child buried without a coffin?)

Names appear of families recorded later, or even today; Hutsons or Hotstons (probably variations of the same name) appear regularly. (See Charles Hotston, below, and Jean Hotston's memories in Chapter 4; she said of her husband 'Fred was Binsted, and Binsted was Fred.') In 1785 '3 Quart faggots with carriage' for William Hotstone cost 15s.; in 1790 'Hutson's Boy was sick'; in 1795 the Ruffs' and Hutsons' house rent was £5.4s.0d. Denyers, a name known later at Meadow Lodge, were given wood and 'necessarys' in 1794, and in 1795 flour and money for rent.

Though the date of building the poorhouse is not recorded, in 1777 there is an entry 'to posts and nails for the poor house and carriage, 10s.6d.' In 1778 'paid Mr Allcock for half a year's interest for money the parishioners hired [this word is unclear] to build the poor house, £1.2s.6d.' In 1779 'to the digging a well at the poor house, £2.2s.0d.' Before the new poorhouse was built (perhaps about 1777), a poorhouse was rented, costing £2 or £3 a year. References to renting a poorhouse continue to 1787.

Other entries record work done; in 1759 'paid Caigers for picking 41 L of stones, £1.0s.6d.'; 'paid Richard Tupper for work done at the Common gate, 2s.6d.' The many entries for pairs of pattens suggest the perennial muddiness of Binsted's lanes – more extreme in those days, as witnessed by the entry in 1761, 'to a tree to lay across the lane, 2s.'

Charlotte Read's painting of the 'Poorhouse' next to Binsted church. Probably built in the 1770s, it was demolished about 1910.

Isaac Rawlins: a sad tale *John Heathcote*

These kinds of historical anecdotes usually relate to the great and the good, but this is the story of a more modest resident of Binsted who lived in the early nineteenth century. The 'Jane Austen' type characters are well-known, because we still have their letters and writings, but the lowlier characters often depicted by Dickens would have been unable to write and their daily lives and characters could only be guessed at; although nowadays someone, somewhere, is probably doing a thesis on the psychology of the Artful Dodger.

Isaac was convicted at Petworth Quarter Sessions on 18th November 1833 aged 48 yrs (a fairly advanced age at that time when his life expectancy would have been less than 50) of stealing 'a piece of beech timber worth 9d' from Ann, Dowager Countess of Newburgh and one foot of timber at 9d from John Gage and Philip Howard. The Countess is shown as being owner of at least part of Binsted Woods on 1825 maps, and the family's arms still adorn the inn at Slindon, where she owned the estate, and had the building which is now the Folly in Eartham Wood built in 1814 as a summerhouse. The other victims of the theft were, from the name, probably connected to the Norfolk Estate.

Isaac was probably the only person from Binsted in that era whose description we have, viz: '5 ft 8 in tall, Stout build, Dark hair, Fresh complexion, Hazel eyes.' He is clearly listed in both his court appearances as coming from Binsted but was almost certainly christened in Slindon, as were his four children. He had a previous conviction (stealing 11 gallons of wheat) from 11 years before but the records do not show if this time he was starving or freezing. For that crime he was given a seven-year transportation sentence. It was relatively unusual (and difficult) for convicts to return having completed their sentence and he may not have gone for some reason.

The outcome was that he was again sentenced to be transported to Australia for seven years, and would have been sent off to the prison hulks (probably in irons) in the Thames or Portsmouth Harbour before being taken to Van Diemen's Land, where there were already 15,000 convicts including 1,800 women and their children. Because of the unpleasant history and probably the unfortunate pun in its name Van Diemen's Land became Tasmania in its centenary year of 1856.

Do you remember Magwitch in Great Expectations who had escaped from a hulk in the Thames and whose harsh sentence was transportation for life? The government policy had originally been, at the turn of the century, to empty the hulks and prisons and settle Australia before the French could do so. Captain Cook had charted the coast in 1770 and the first convict settlers and guards arrived, not knowing what to expect, in 1788 and had difficulty in staving off starvation.

A four-month journey in the hold of a small wooden ship across the oceans, with minimal food and medicine, would have been sufficient punishment for Isaac's crime in itself and worse than almost any sentence today. The contracting ship-owners were paid for the numbers of convicts leaving England rather than those landing in Australia. But as Brenda Dixon points out in her book on Walberton, the regulations protecting the voyaging convicts were stronger than those for the free emigrants. By 1833 only a small number of deaths occurred among the 300 or so prisoners on each ship as against 17% in one of the early fleets.

Living conditions in the countryside in Sussex at this time were bad following the introduction of machines. A threat to farm workers' livelihoods (wages were 50-70p per week) was posed by the introduction of threshing machines. Riots, Luddite-style damage to machinery and rick burning were common throughout the south and south-east, inflamed by the mythical Captain Swing whose name appeared on threatening letters to unjust employers. The name 'Swing' came from part of the flail which was used to thresh the corn manually during winter when there was no work in the fields.

A number of local men were transported, especially from the Westbourne-Fishbourne-Pagham area, which would have been a major corn-growing area. They were later pardoned but only about 10% returned – why should they, considering the conditions they had left? Records of the convicts, their voyages, and what happened to them were remarkably well-documented, given the conditions, the illiteracy of the prisoners and the level of penmanship of their captors, and many of them were released through a parole system and eventually freed to become successful citizens (like Magwitch).

Although Isaac Rawlins is not listed on the Tasmanian Archives web-site under the name of Isaac it must be more than coincidence that one 'John' Rawlins, born in the same year (1785), died without children or siblings in Tasmania in 1836 aged 51 which, given the kind of life he must have led, was a reasonable age for the time.

The Reads of Binsted House

Ann Staker died in 1840 without children, and left Binsted House together with much of Binsted (and Stakers Farm at Southwater, Horsham) to Harry Read, the son of her elder sister Frances Read. Harry farmed at West Dean and did not take up residence at Binsted. However he implemented protracted renovations to the property, starting in 1840. These were not completed until the year after his death in 1848. In 1849 (on completion of the renovations) his son William Henry Read (1822-1888), who was known as 'the 8th Squire', married Sarah Walburn (1823-1907) and moved into Binsted House.

Remarkably, some vivid personal memories of this family have survived to the present day. The link was an interview in 1994 with Henry Pethers of Binsted (1914-1996). Henry Pethers had come to Binsted in 1928 when his family took over the Black Horse pub. They also ran a shop and bakery, and had run the London and County Stores in Walberton for four years. The family had moved from London in

Wednesday July 13th, 1898, at Binsted Rectory near Arundel, Sussex: wedding of Charles Read of Binsted House and Florence Lewis of the Rectory. Florence wrote the caption: 'Left to right, standing: Mr. C. Green, Leslie Lewis, Helen Miller, Edwin Ellis, Kathleen Lewis, Minnie Read, Mansel Lewis, Judy Lewis, Edgar Lewis, Doug Read, Mrs. Graburn, Dr.Green, Mrs Izard, Mitchell Ellis, Rev Izard, Uncle Ned Miller, Mabel Lewis with Vivien Lewis (baby), George Tanner. Left to right, sitting: Mother, Annie Read, Edie Lewis, Norah Lewis, Bridegroom and Bride (CER and FMCR), Ted Read, Fan Read, Mrs Crowley, Miss Hollis, Father, Newton Lewis, Emily Lewis, William Read.'

1924, when Henry was ten, to help his mother get over the death of her daughter Doris. In 1939 Mr Pethers married Margaret Ernestine Read, known as Kitty, born in 1899. She was the only child of the marriage in 1898 between Charles Ernest Read, youngest of eight children of the William and Sarah Read of Binsted House, and Florence Lewis, one of thirteen children of the Rector of Binsted, Henry Lewis (1830-1907). The wedding is captured in a splendid group photograph taken on the Rectory Lawn by the Rev. Lewis's son Henry.

Mrs Pethers' memory of her grandmother, Sarah Read, was that she 'sailed like a barge' in her vast bombazine dresses and 'never did anything'. Sarah's sister, Hannah, had lost all her money and came to live at Binsted House as a 'lady's companion' and much-valued aunt. William and Sarah had four sons and four daughters. They were Charlotte or Lottie; Annie, Fanny and Minnie; Edward Staker, William or Wig, Harry or Doug, and Charles Ernest (Mrs Pethers' father). The Staker name was customarily used by the eldest son in the family.

Edward Staker Read, Mrs Pethers' 'Uncle Ted', was known as 'the Squire' or 'the 9th Squire', and lived at Binsted House after his father's death in 1888. He was known as 'Edward Staker'. Like his father, he was a JP. He used to say that his father, William Henry, once saw

Read family group at Binsted House, c. 1880. Back row, left to right: Harry Douglas Read, two friends of the family, Edward Staker Read, Charles Read. Front row, left to right: William Walburn Read, Fanny Jane Read, Mr William Henry Read, Mrs Sarah Read, Minnie S. Read and Charlotte Sarah Read.

poachers, chased them with his gun, firing and reloading as he went, stopped them and caught them, took them to Arundel and charged them himself. His gun was a muzzle-loader, made in Arundel. 'You had to look out when ramming powder and shot down, as the muzzle would cut you. The muzzles were made out of horseshoe nails, often called 'Damascus steel'. There was a walnut tree up at the house – all old houses had one; when your eldest son was born a sapling was planted, and when he was twenty-one a gun was made with walnut wood from the tree for the butt.'

'Uncle Ted' (1857-1924) lived the life of a squire and kept a hunter and groom. The groom's name was Styles; he lived at Morley's Croft and was paid a pension until he died. 'Some of the housemaids that were venturesome used to get up at four in the morning and bribe the grooms to let them ride the hunters.' The other boys were all apprenticed to someone; there was 'string-pulling even in those days'. Doug went into the tea business in Mincing Lane. It was possible to commute to London – you walked through the woods to Ford Station. Wig disgraced himself (he had a drink problem) and was 'rusticated down in the country. He spent most of his time in the harness room. It was a nice room and never leaked, and was well locked up.' He helped run the farms on the estate.

A nice insight into Edward Staker Read and his knowledge of bees comes from the diary of Laurence Graburn, a local farmer, passed on via his daughter to Clifford Blakey of Havenwood Park. Mr Graburn wrote:

Mr E.S.Read of Binsted was a great bee-man and had as many as 110 stocks in the wood adjourning his house. As a young man he worked in the Bank of England, but when 21 was sent home in galloping consumption, this did not kill him, and though never robust he lived to 67.

I met him on horseback once riding through Arundel to the Station, he told me I am going to do a thing I have never done before, viz: I am going to order a truck for a ton of honey. This sounds a lot but it was a honey year and would only be a portion of his takings that summer.

I saw Mr Read do the smartest thing I ever saw, he had imported some Italian Queens as an experiment and when I went there one day he showed me a very strong stock he expected to swarm, he had introduced an Italian Queen into it. After watching it for a while we went into lunch, leaving his man to keep an eye on them, we had not been there long when the man came to say they had swarmed and were going away, neither Mr Read nor his man were very agile so I ran out and was able to follow them for a while, but could not keep up. The last I saw of them they were flying towards Dick Denyer's house [Meadow Lodge].

I searched this with no result when I met Mr Read just arriving, we then saw Denyer very excited, who told us a huge swarm had settled in a Plum tree in his garden. Mr Read assured him they were his bees, but Denyer would not part as he had kept bees before and his sisters wanted him to start again. We then watched Denyer take them, and as often happens a few returned to the bough, Mr Read looked at the little cluster and quickly picked one off and put it in a match box, he had the Italian Queen and in a few seconds the air was full of bees again, and Mr Read told Denyer he would have to take them again, but they would not stay as he had the Queen in his pocket. The bees not finding the Queen returned to their old hive, and Denyer very upset at losing them.

Charles Ernest Read (1862-1939) went into Denny's bacon firm in London as a clerk in the office. During the First World War, women went into munitions and then into office jobs, and clerks were sacked, including him. 'He was very much against women taking men's jobs.' He lived at Penge near Crystal Palace in London. Later, after his marriage to Florence Lewis, with her dowry they took a boarding house at Dalgeny Mount near Ventnor in the Isle of Wight. There was a constant stream of visitors coming for holidays, so well-known to the family that 'to me they sounded more like relatives'.

Charles insisted on calling Mr Pethers Harry, not Henry. 'He didn't agree with Uncle Henry, so I was called Harry, like it or lump it. I remember him saying of someone that he was a very short man, but he himself was 18 inches shorter than me. He didn't think he was short. No short man ever thinks he's short; just other people are too bloody long!'

'Miss Lottie' and her sisters

Miss Lottie, or Charlotte Sarah Read (1850-1943), known by Mrs Pethers as 'Aunt Tot', was the oldest of the family and used to say she should have had the property. 'If you see one of the servants running with her apron over her head, crying her eyes out, she's just met Miss Lottie. They say she used to put on a man's hat and do the flues.' In old age she lost all her hair and was bed-ridden. 'She used to sit up in bed and bang her stick and give orders. I never saw Miss Lottie and I don't think I missed much.' However, she did some notable paintings of Binsted, and ensured her place in local history by making a drawing of the interior of Binsted Church as it was before the 'Restoration' in 1868 – box pews, gallery, grinding organ and all.

Charlotte Read.

Her obituary gave a kinder picture of her. 'Nothing made her more happy than to talk of the times she had enjoyed in the old house, with its beautiful park and woodlands, and of the walks and picnics with her brothers and sisters in the neighbouring district…Her love of animals remained with her, and a few hours before her death a black cat, which she called her 'boon companion', was to be seen on her bed. Miss Read remembered the times when labour was very cheap. Women would work for 6d. a day in the house and the average labourer's wage was 12s. a week. Messages and carriage of parcels were paid for by drinks of good ale, then to be bought for 8d. a gallon…Although bedridden for over 12 years, she was always cheerful and patient…She much admired the writings of Dean Inge, and she would chat upon his teaching most readily…No terrors of modern warfare could frighten this fine old lady as she lay serenely in her quiet room. Those who knew her will long remember with affection her quick humour, kindly disposition, and sincerity': another way of describing bluntness and a sharp tongue.

Annie, or Anna Maria Read, died in 1900 aged 46. She was a great gardener, and it was thought she got cancer from it. Miss Fanny 'went a bit funny' as a girl and spent some time in an asylum. She was deaf (apparently deafness ran in the family), and spoke in an odd way, but was musical and used to play the organ in Binsted Church. She used to bang on the door of the church, or on the Rectory door, and ask to speak to 'William' (Drury, the Rector). She was a problem to look after, always in trouble for breaking things. Her care was a big expense to the family, and 'pulled them down'. 'You'd lose sight of her and she'd be gone, out of the front door. You'd go after her and find one galosh in the lane.'

Her mental problems continued. 'When Miss Fanny poked her umbrella through the window pane in her bedroom I got up a ladder and mended it. She poked the panes out on purpose; she thought I was Mr Upton (Sid Upton, who farmed at Marsh Farm) or his ghost. He had auburn hair, the same as mine was before it went grey. Though what Mr Upton was doing up a ladder mending a window I don't know. As fast as I mended the pane she would poke her umbrella through another one.'

The eccentricities of the three old ladies, and perhaps the black cat, may have been the genesis of a Binsted myth. Paul Wyatt, whose family farmed in Walberton, remembers that in the 1930s his father rented land at Binsted Park as pasture for heifers and some sheep. 'Behind the house was a stable yard with some loose boxes, which we used occasionally for sick heifers. The first time my brother and I went into this yard we saw three 'witches' brooms' leaning against a wall. This made a good story to tell at the next mealtime. We rarely saw the sisters, but when we did they were always dressed in black, with little showing except their hands. After a few years one of them died and we noticed soon afterwards that one of the brooms had gone. That didn't wait long for an opportunity at the meal-table.' This must have been Miss Fanny, who died in 1936, aged 83. Minnie died in 1939, aged 75.

Binsted House

Binsted House has now been demolished. After the First World War, there was a decline in income from the land, so that the Read family had to sell off property in order to live. There was no money to repair the house, and Charles Read and his wife Florence built a new house, the Manor House, nearby in 1924. Ralph Ellis, a noted sign-painter, painted Binsted House in a ruinous state in the 1940s, overgrown with creepers and with glass missing from the windows. The handsome stables, and the ruins of the house, remained until recently. There is planning permission for a large house on the site.

As part of the planning permission, excavations were done in August 2000, which established 'with some degree of certainty that the core of the house was an L-shaped building of late 17th or early 18th century date, added to in several stages in the 18th and 19th centuries, with a service range of c. 1800. The separate flint-built stables and coach house were…mid-19th-century in date, not 17th-century as suggested in 1998' (letter from John Mills, County Archaeologist). They were made with re-used older bricks. Counting the rings of an oak which grew by the ha-ha, blown down in 1987, gave a date of 1760-1770 for the ha-ha, which divided the garden from the pasture or field and kept livestock out without spoiling the view.

According to an archaeological survey of the ruins in 1998, a map of 1778 (Yeakell

Binsted House painted by Ralph Ellis in 1946.

and Gardner) shows the house enclosed in a large rectangle, surrounded to the north, south and west by woodland, with an east vista giving a clear view to the river Arun. A track which has now disappeared ran north-south through the woodland west of the house. By 1825 the woodland to the south had largely been cleared and the southern and western vistas of the Park opened up. Windows on the east side had been blocked, perhaps because of the window tax introduced in 1745, while those on the south side were left. This enabled enjoyment of a new view and gave full benefit of the sun.

Mrs Pethers remembered being told that the imposing 'false front' had been added to the house in the eighteenth century, giving it a carriage sweep and a porticoed doorway with windows on either side – actually French windows opening like doors, facing away from Binsted Lane and onto the Park. Mr Pethers remembered: 'As you entered the hall you saw stairs rising in front of you then turning right at a landing. At the turn of the stairs was the only lavatory in the house. Over the hallway was a glass dome that let light into the hall.' This may have been the feature behind stories of a 'minstrel's gallery'. 'All work on the house was done by local tradesmen from Arundel, who came on penny-farthing bicycles, or estate workers. The work was crude and rough – there was no beautiful furniture. It was a well-known fact that horses were better looked after than human beings.'

The two main front rooms on either side of the hall were the drawing-room and the dining-room. Over each was a bedroom: one Miss Lottie's and one Miss Fanny's. 'Old Miss Lottie didn't like men. She wouldn't have allowed me there in any case. So I didn't go into the bedrooms.' There was a still room under the stairs to the left of the hall, and opposite on the right was the nursery. In front of you was a door to the cellar. The nursery had its own door to the outside, to the nursery lawn on the right hand side of the house.

On the left, past the still room, was a huge scullery. It had a water pump and Mr

A Victorian photograph of the stable block at Binsted House. Fire destroyed the roof in the early 1950s. The building was recently demolished.

Pethers used to pump up water for the old ladies. There were stone sinks and a back door to the dairy, a single-storey room with thick slate worktops where butter was made with milk from the cows. Opposite the dairy was the bakery, with an oven in the corner, and tacked on the end was a harness room. Beyond the 'nursery lawn' was a glasshouse. There was a hatch into the coal cellar (which was above ground) from Binsted Lane, with a hook in the wall for the coalman's horse to be attached to.

There were small upstairs rooms for servants at the back of the house, poky and odd-shaped, with sloping ceilings. There were back stairs leading to a passageway – these stairs were not safe to walk up in Mrs Pethers' time. Another small staircase led from one servant's bedroom to an attic. 'That's where the scullery maid was pushed. She was the first to get up in the morning and give everybody tea.'

Outside there were granary stones, a cider press in the 'hovels' or open-fronted sheds in the courtyard, 'pigsties', and a garden off to the left. 'They were going to wall it all the way round, but they ran out of money.' There was a summerhouse, a beehouse on the lawn, a pond garden, and three ponds (the middle one still exists as the 'Madonna pond'). The toilets and drains all drained into the 'Pond garden' under the road.

There were wells 'all over the show' (though only two were found in the excavations). Mr Pethers used to draw two buckets of water from the well at the side of the house for the two old ladies. At that time people often thought the water was bad; if two or three children died, they blamed the water. 'Well's bad. Just lost mother and granny don't look so good. Need a new well.' They would dig a new well, near the old one, and often did not bother to fill the old one in. One well at Binsted House had rusty water: it was so brown that when one of the boys was a baby people used to think he had 'khaki napkins'. The northernmost of the three ponds always had rusty water and was known as 'the iron-bound pond'.

Bill Pethers, the son of Henry Pethers and Margaret Read, added the following rider to this account of the Read family and his father's memories:

I think my father only saw my great-aunts in their final years and remembered them as old and lonely ladies. My late mother, being that much older (15 years) than my father, often related her fond memories of her aunts, who she said were both kind and caring people, who loved music, painting and the countryside. I remember from my childhood the drawing room at the front of the house had an upright piano in it and several violins and piles of music. I am sure that my mother inherited these attributes from the Read side of the family. My grandfather, Charles Read, whom I never met, was described as a kind and courteous gentleman, with a good sense of humour, who made welcome all who obeyed the rules of the countryside. If you worked for the Reads you were not well paid, but you were respected and cared for like one of the family.

If the Read family had a failing, it was their naivety in the fast and changing world around them, that was so different from the peace and isolation of Binsted Park. They were, after all, born in a different age, now almost forgotten.

William Henry Read Pethers

Jane Caseley's letters

Jane Caseley, born Laker, was for seven years housekeeper to her aunt Ann Staker at Binsted House, before she died in 1840. Jane left Binsted for the USA in 1844. In 1870 and 1888 she wrote to William Henry Read from Knightstown, Indiana. Her first letter thanks him for his kindness to her husband, Mr Caseley, who had been visiting Binsted, and continues: 'He thought as almost everyone does that Binsted is one of the most delightful spots he ever saw. The holly he brought I planted in a box. I think it will grow. I hold it almost sacred. The leaves of the carnation I have pressed in a book to preserve them, the sight of which brings to my mind many recollections of past joys and sorrows. Binsted is the place where I spent the longest time of my life; although a disinterested person I cannot help feeling attached to it. The changes are great indeed, but not more so than I might expect. It is twenty-seven years since I left. But really which seems to surprise me the most is yourself having a family of eight children! It appears as almost yesterday when you was only a small boy, and used to run around fishing and other amusements, and sometimes you used to get hungry and ask me for something to eat when you did not want your Aunt Nancy to see you. The last recollection is you were a young Gent just left school, and going on visits to Mr Palmer…did you ever get your silk cradle quilt Mrs Johnson of Yapton was to make for you? If so you have some pieces of my dress in it. I was truly happy to learn you enjoys Binsted so much, and I sincerely hope many blessings may attend you and yours.'

In 1888 she wrote again, to thank William Henry Read for sending a photograph of Binsted House – perhaps one of the ones we have, taken by Henry Lewis, son of the Rector. 'On our return home, your kind remembrance of me and happy greeting in the sight of the dear old place Binsted House; I cannot express how grateful it is to my feelings to know you have not forgotten me. Please accept my best thanks. I could scarcely stop from viewing, it all looked so natural, the old cherry tree still there, and everything around appears so beautiful. I think I can recognise the old pigeon house peering through the evergreens, and harmless sheep grazing. But what a pleasing addition, I thought, had yourself

Jane Caseley and family.

and family been standing on the green, where the sheep looks so large that I could have had a look at you. However, the view as it is looks beautiful. Mr Caseley tells me he believes my eyesight is benefited by looking at it so much.'

Of his eight children, she writes: 'But the little ones then I trust are all grown up, with the elder ones in love and a great comfort to their parents. Such is life and the changes which naturally takes place.' In fact, none of the four girls married, and only two of the boys. The only child of the eight was Mrs Pethers, daughter of Charles Ernest. Jane Caseley continues: 'I have to tell you of one of our American wonders. Have you heard of our finding natural gas, by going down into the bowels of the earth for it? This winter we have been supplied with natural gas for all cooking and heating purposes as well as the rooms lighted.' She explains how it is found by boring eight or twelve hundred feet below ground: 'As soon as they find it they 'shoot the well' as they call it with some combustibles, when up comes the gas in a full flame of light which can be seen many miles around, till it is confined and conducted into pipes to supply the town.'

A third letter from her which exists was addressed to Sarah Read, and was probably sent after the death of William Henry Read in 1888, as a result of Sarah asking for information about the Staker family. Jane Caseley comments on the lives and deaths of Ann Staker's nine brothers and sisters and remembers the burial of 'Aunt Nancy' (Ann Staker) in the vault in the chancel of Binsted church in 1840. 'I looked in the Sunday after her funeral and saw it was not very deep.'

The Lewises of the Rectory

The Lewis family at the Rectory had no money problems, even with thirteen children. Henry Lewis, the Rector, who built the Rectory in the 1860s, had in 1856 married an heiress, Edith Miller. He changed his name, Bones, to Lewis in 1869. Their daughters had a dowry of £7,000 each. Florence, their fourth child, Mrs Pethers' mother, 'always used to think she married beneath her in marrying the Squire's son from Binsted House,'

Lewis family group taken at Binsted Rectory c. 1880. Some of the Lewis family trying their best to remain motionless for the long exposures required for a camera of the day. The purpose of the white sheet was probably to augment the background light.
Left to right, back row: Bingley Cass, Norah Lewis, Henry Lewis (photographer), Christine Lewis.
Middle row: Revd. Henry Lewis, Emily Lewis, Mrs Edith Lewis, Kathleen Lewis (on lap). Front row: Florence, Mary, Mansel and Edith Lewis.

remembered Mr Pethers. 'She always used to ram in the Rectory – wonderful Rectory – wonderful Father and Mother.' She wore her hair in the 'Princess Alexandra style', with extra hair she used to pad in. 'Women are judged by their legs now; in those days it was by the amount of hair they had. There was yards and yards of horsehair in their buns.' In many photos Florence is wearing beautiful lacy blouses, hats and jewellery.

There was intense competition within this large family. 'The rows that went on! The hair that was pulled out!' One area of competition was who had the best garden. Each year a big box of

Members of the Lewis family relaxing on the Rectory lawn.

seeds was sent for, and vegetable seeds were handed out to the brothers-in-law to grow in their gardens. Among the sisters, 'If X wrote to Y saying something unflattering about Z (such as "She's put on a lot of weight lately") Y might well write to Z and enclose the unflattering letter from X'. But one of the boys, known as 'darling Leslie', had an angelic face and curls. His space in the linen press with a named space for each child was named 'Darling Leslie'.

'Darling Leslie' on the bridge over Binsted Rife.

The Rector and the 'restoration'

The Rector of Binsted was a strong-minded man – as is apparent from the churchwardens' accounts and 'vestry meeting' minute books in the W.S.R.O. The accounts for 1868 record two separate rates being made, one for the 'repair' of the church, one for the 'restoration'. The rate for the 'repair' was made 'the third day of April, 1868, at one shilling in the £' and raised £44.18s.18 1/2d. Presumably most parishioners paid. The rate for the 'restoration' raised £80, but this was paid entirely by four people. 'Only Montifeore Esqr Mr Upton Mr Read and E Ellis paid their portion of the Rate in the subscription towards the Restoration of the Church'. A table shows Mr Upton paid £40, Mr Read £15, Montifeore Esq £5, and E. Ellis £20.

The two rates reflect a disagreement about whether the church should be 'repaired and restored', which was what the Rector wanted, or only 'repaired', which was what the other members of the vestry meeting wanted, and, it seems, most of the parishioners. We know this from the record of the vestry meeting of 2 April 1868. 'It was proposed by the Rector that the church be repaired and restored. Mr Upton moved as an amendment that the words 'and restored' do not form part of the question. Mr Upton, Mr Read, Mr Ellis for the amendment. But H.C.Bones [the Rector] for the original

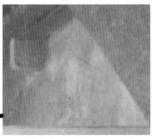

Part of the lost wall painting of Christ's enthronement?

This photograph of the inside of Binsted church probably dates from 1877 (a companion photograph of the graveyard shows the new grave of Thomas Denyer, who died that year). The smart new rood screen, pews and pulpit were put in by the Rev. Henry Lewis in 1867-8. In 1867 mediaeval wall paintings were found preserved under whitewash all over the church, but had gone by 1888. Possible traces of the paintings are visible in this photograph over the rood screen on the right, on the south chancel wall, where the entombment and enthronement of Christ were depicted.

proposition. The amendment was therefore carried. Authority was then given to the churchwarden to make a rate for the necessary repairs of the nave of the church.'

But in June the Rector got his way. At stake was a plan to strip out the Georgian interior fittings of the church (box pews, gallery, three-decker pulpit and texts) and replace them with a 'high church' interior, as described in Chapter 1. At a vestry meeting on 6 June, 'the following resolution was submitted to the meeting, 'that Mr Bones's plan as suggested by the Architect Mr Jackson, and submitted to this meeting, for the Restoration of the church should be adopted, Mr Bones taking upon himself the entire outlay and completion of the works, on the Parish meeting placing in his hands the sum of 80 pounds towards such an outlay; the allotment of pews to follow the existing order as far as possible.' In the face of this offer, the vestry meeting gave in, and the 'restoration' went ahead.

Miss Charlotte Read's drawing of how the church was fitted out before the 'restoration' can be seen as part of this controversy. Her father, William Henry Read, was one of the unwilling vestry meeting members who eventually paid up. The fact that her picture carefully records what pews belonged to whom suggests that the 'allotment of pews' was an important matter. However, uncertainties in her drawing such as question marks, and a redrafted outline for one of the box pews, suggest it may have been made later, rather than at the time of the restoration.

A further twist is given to the story by the fact that at the time of the restoration, mediaeval wall paintings were discovered all over the walls of the church, which had been hidden by being painted over at the Reformation. These were written up excitedly in the journal *Sussex Archaeological Collections*, in 1868, but a few years later (1888) had perished – all except the now very faded painting (of St Margaret or Mary – or St Ambrose? See above) in the window splay. The 1868 article, by C.S.Leslie of 'Slyndon House', said: 'The great interest of Binsted, however, arises from the beautiful and perfect mural paintings, both figures and decorations, which seem entirely to cover the church. Those discovered by Mr Jackson, under whose care the restoration will be conducted, are on the north and south chancel walls, and at the south door. The whitewash comes off with unusual ease, but no further uncovering will be allowed till the heavy parts of the restoration are done, for fear of injury…' (SAC, Vol. XX, 1868, p. 233). It is notable that this article was written before the restoration, but when it was in prospect, and the paintings had only been partly uncovered - possibly before the meetings described above.

No-one knows what happened to the paintings. An article dated 1888 in SAC (Vol. XLIII, 1900, p. 225) says 'On the S. Chancel wall were the Entombment and the Enthronement…there was also a painting by the S. door of the nave, subject unrecorded…All these were allowed to perish at the time.' The existing painting is very fragile (at one time, before yet another restoration, the paint seemed to be held on by cobwebs) and it is easy to believe they might have perished by accident. But it is tempting to speculate about the new desire to 'clean' the church after the restoration. The Parish Clerk was paid 10s a year to cover this in 1869, 1870, 1873-6, and 1883, though he seems to have paid someone else to do it and wash the surplice. After 1883, no more mention is made of money for cleaning the church. Before the restoration, cleaning the church is not mentioned – just 'cleaning church path'. Perhaps somebody scrubbed too hard, either by mistake, or because of dislike of the new arrangements.

Kents and Denyers

On 23 August 1908, a purse of money and a beautifully written citation were presented to Mr and Mrs Stephen Kent, of Kent's cottage in Binsted Park, on their Golden Wedding day by the parishioners of Binsted. Seventy-six people are listed as having 'much pleasure in presenting you with the accompanying Purse as a small token of our esteem and regard on the occasion of your Golden Wedding, and in appreciation of the excellent manner in which you (Mr Kent) have carried out your duties of Parish Clerk during a period of 39

Mr and Mrs Stephen Kent.

years.'   Many Reads and Lewises are named, also Mr and Mrs Alfred Hotston, and Mr Alfred Hotston Junior.

Another contributor was Mr Richard B. Denyer or Dickie Denyer of Meadow Lodge, mentioned above.   He and his sister farmed at Meadow Lodge for over 60 years and were remembered fondly in the Women's Institute scrapbook of 1947.   J.Mansell wrote: 'Their wisdom, their humour and the beauty of these wonderful old people cannot be described…I shall never forget seeing Miss Denyer coming home in deep snow one morning after an all-night vigil by an old lady's beside.   She was exhausted, and yet for a whole winter she repeated that labour of love, and I think very few people knew of it.'

Dickie Denyer is also remembered by Paul Wyatt of Walberton.   'He was a tall, dignified old man who was always charming and polite to everyone, and that included his few cows which he used to watch over as they grazed beside the road.   When his cows had had their fill of the grass beside the road, he escorted them back to his paddock or to the cow-house.   He rarely let his cows graze near to the Park gate but if one of them ever did, it provoked Mr. Read to wrath and he was quickly on the warpath.   Mr. Read took his dignified politeness for submission.'

Harold Dean and the Great War   *Beryl House*

In 1830 Charles Hotston (Charles I) was baptised in Binsted.   He had eleven children; one of them, Emma (1866-1950), married Henry Dean, and their son Harold Dean (1894-1929) had a daughter, now Beryl House (b. 1923), who has written about her family and in particular her grandmother Emma.

According to church records, Charles I, Emma's father, was born in 1830 at Binsted, the son of James Hudston and his wife Harriet.   James Hudston was born in 1795 and the Binsted records name his father as being one William Hudson, born in 1753, who in turn possibly could have been the son of one Thomas Husher or Usher and his wife Mary; but the ancient records are hard to decipher and not very explicit.   The gradual change in the surname was probably because the persons concerned could neither read nor write and the only clerk was probably the incumbent who wrote down the names phonetically in an effort to keep a record.   If the subjects had thick country accents, not easily understood, these would quite likely have resulted in the gradual change of name.

Charles Hotston was landlord of the 'Sir George Thomas' Arms' (or 'the Spur') at Slindon for 52 years.

Coppicing in Binsted Woods.

Whilst also a wood merchant he no doubt used the abundant wood growing in the area as well as at nearby Binsted from where he had originated. Binsted Woods in my early days were let out by their owner(s) for rent to be coppiced and husbanded correctly. The tenant sold the woody produce of his hard labours as logs for fires cut from large branches, bean poles from long straight sticks and faggots made from brushwood tips. Nothing was wasted and after coppicing the resultant new growth could be used all over again and again in eleven year cycles. Faggots were in great demand for pea sticks as well as for kindling for fires and in bakers' ovens. The faggots, or bundles, were burnt in the long ovens, which had a regulated draught and were vented at the far end to remove the smoke. Then the ashes were raked out forwards and the loaves inserted on a long spatula in their place. The resulting loaf was delicious as the crust had absorbed the taste of the burnt wood – something which has never been simulated by any other later method of baking.

After her marriage to Henry Dean on 1st February 1893, Emma continued her duties at the pub and they both lived there. Their first child, Harold, my father, was born in the third bedroom from the left on 19th September, 1894. He was apparently a very bright child and when he was only three years old he was sent to school in the village. On the first day he attended Emma walked with him across the fields from the pub. However, he refused to let her meet him afterwards and insisted on returning home by himself. Emma was worried so watched out for him from the pub and was greatly relieved to see him coming in the distance. She dared not let him see her but went forward to meet him at the very last moment. He was in great form and thrilled by his achievement.

Emma watched her children grow up to become responsible citizens. Harold worked hard to become a fully qualified electrical and mechanical engineer while Lena was apprenticed to millinery. Absorbed by all of the then modern techniques Harold installed a simple form of electricity in the family home. At that time Littlehampton was not served with electricity but there was coal gas which their house used for lighting and some of the cooking in an early black cast iron gas stove. During the colder months the kitchener stove took care of all cooking and heating of the kitchen. Harold's electrical system provided light only and was run by a small petrol engine mounted on a huge stone block in the garden shed. The stone was large enough to allow a big fly-wheel, which was about the diameter of a large bicycle wheel and which projected out over the side of it, to revolve when the engine was going. It was run for a short time each day and the electricity produced was stored in a large accumulator in readiness for being drawn upon when the lights were used in the house.

It was on the 3rd August, 1914, and just before Harold's 20th birthday, that disaster struck when England and Germany commenced hostilities. The Great War of 1914-1918 had begun. Along with most of his friends Harold joined up and went to war, leaving his mother in charge of the electrical arrangements. Daily she faithfully set it going and when he returned home for leave from France he saw that it was maintained until eventually it had to be given up and the house reverted back to the exclusive use of gas.

During his army service in France Harold was in the Royal Ordnance Corps and became an 'artificer', that is 'a soldier mechanic', attached to the ordnance, artillery and engineer service. He was skilled in sending and receiving messages in both semaphore and Morse codes. He rode a horse and with others was responsible for the movement of the big guns which in those days were horse-drawn on special carriages. Pitted by shell holes, the muddy terrain of Northern France during the terrible trench warfare was extremely treacherous, and Harold's horse slipped, threw him and then rolled on him, breaking his leg. This accident brought about a spell in hospital back in England or 'Blighty' as it was known to the soldiers. While in hospital the walking patients wore bright blue uniforms which they also called 'Blighty'. Wearing wet clothes and sleeping in damp blankets in France brought on an attack of pleurisy which meant another spell of 'Blighty'. Eventually he recovered, but it left what was called a 'spot' on his lung.

After the Great War ended on 11th November, 1918, Harold was eventually demobilised from the army in 1919, but not before he had won a number of trophies for rifle shooting. These were two silver plated tankards, awarded to 'Corporal Dean, Nov. 6 1918', when after hospitalisation he was transferred to No. 1 Reserve Motor Transport Depot, Grove Park, and again to 'Sergeant Dean, Feb. 1919'. He later won six silver teaspoons, singly, after joining the Miniature Rifle Club Society. He was disappointed that the pretty delicate design of the first two was changed so that all six were not alike. He had great accuracy, became a 'crack shot' and his exploits entitled him to shoot at Bisley.

Emma was very proud of him and was delighted when he married May Burch in 1920. She was devastated by his untimely death in 1929, from tuberculosis, when I was only just six years old. She took great comfort from the fact that his last resting place was in Littlehampton cemetery which she could easily visit.

'Binsted is on strike': 1937

A planning battle from the past, which gives us a rich description of Binsted in the 1930s and some of its personalities, is introduced with these words in the Southern Weekly News, Saturday, 22 May, 1937.

It has been waged for four years and it will go on to the bitter end…Binsted, quiet Sussex backwater, tiny village of twisting lanes, trim hedgerows, is on strike…Binsted people mean to fight to keep the name of Binsted alive, to continue their struggle now waged for four years against the West Sussex County Council.

It was in 1933 that the County Council issued the order that the parish of Binsted should be added to the parish of Tortington, a village three miles away. For four years Binsted has refused to ackowledge this change, has stuck more firmly to its own village life, ignored sleepy-eyed Tortington even more than Tortington ignores Binsted.

Binsted people will not walk to Tortington for a Parish meeting. Tortington will not come to Binsted. Attempts made to hold a meeting on neutral ground has failed because both sides, by mutual consent, adjourn the meeting almost before it begins, make no decisions.

They call it a strike in Binsted, a strike that has been waged for years but today is reaching a climax. Both the Rector, the Rev. William Drury, and Mr S.H.Upton, genial farmer whose family has farmed on the land in Binsted since 1500, told me that it was a strike – and a strike to the bitter end.

The Rector was indignant. As he put it in the article: 'Fancy asking our people to walk three miles to a parish meeting! It is impossible to work with Tortington. It is a matter I am very hot about. The real union would be if Arundel took over Tortington and Binsted was joined to Walberton [as eventually happened in the 1980s], or else, better still, leave us alone… We used to enjoy our parish meetings so much, too. We could all meet and see each other and talk over matters. Now all that is lost.'

Mr Upton is quoted as giving some good reasons why the two parishes do not blend.

'Binsted does not want Tortington and Tortington does not want Binsted. There's the whole problem… Now, Binsted and Tortington have no common interests. Take the Coronation: Binsted had its own show, a great show. We collected £46, had fireworks and plenty of prizes. Because the weather spoilt part of the show on Wednesday we had another Coronation Day last Saturday – with another supper, more fireworks: the whole programme over again! We had a grand time.

'But Tortington did nothing at all. They went in with Arundel and enjoyed their celebrations. You see Tortington is like Arundel. It is owned by the Duke of Norfolk and the people are tenants, while we in Binsted have our own farms and holdings and we are proud of our inheritance. We strongly object to being taken over like this; we refuse to be obliterated. So we are on strike and we refuse to do anything.'

The only dissenting voice quoted is that of Ernest Wishart, of Marsh Farm. He said: 'You see, Binsted does not really exist as a parish now…the sooner we face that fact the better.' He had a more world-wide perspective. Asked about tales of Spanish refugees in the village, he said: 'I have had some of my own friends staying here who had to leave Spain in a hurry. And if I can do anything to help any more who want to find rest here I shall certainly be glad to.'

The article returns to Mr Upton, to describe the contents of an old chest the reporter is shown. 'Parish records of Binsted' are described, possibly the 'Poor Books' now in the Record Office, which were donated by him. 'Famous old documents of a great-grandfather of Mr Upton, musty documents telling of voyages in old sailing ships – dim memories of the pioneer days of the East India Company. For that Mr Upton was skipper of the East India boat Glatton in years round about 1812 and here are his ship's logs telling of adventurous days afloat, of smuggling and greater mysteries.' Mr Upton shows off his racing donkeys, and the article concludes with an atmospheric description of Binsted as a rural backwater.

There is no way out of Binsted except by the way you come. Binsted is a cul-de-sac, and its seclusion breathes everywhere. Rich hedgerows and silent woods are around you. There are no shops…This tree-entwined village has peace with its isolation. Roads twist in too many S-bends for there to be any need for speed limits. And few cars ever come here to churn the dust of the ancient lanes.

Most of the water is drawn from the wells, oil lamps are still used. Binsted could have both modern means, I suppose, without much ado, but they prefer the old ways to the new. The church, with its oil lamps, must be one of the tiniest in

84 AND ACTIVE

His address is Ellcome, Binsted Park. 84 years-old Henry Ell-come keeps active. When not gardening he continues the thatching of his quaint old cottage which has no name.

Mr Ellcombe mending the roof of his cottage, on the site of the present Kent's Cottage.

Sussex. It has a quaint air as you see it from the roadway, the thick high grass flung forward like waves by the wind, a tin cowl at the west end merrily twirling around.

We went in…on the harmonium we found a bunch of sweet peas dipped in what we believe was a pint tankard. It was all so pleasantly informal. Services are not held on Sunday evenings, except on the first Sunday. Evensong, instead, is held at three o'clock. 'It is dark here in the winter,' I was told, 'and the people prefer the afternoon service. We have always had it and we see no need to change.'

Rambling roses grow round the church door. And here you will find a peace broken only by the wind which sweeps through the tall grass of the churchyard, rushes on down the slopes below.

An inset describes Henry Ellcombe, aged 84, of Binsted Park. He lives in 'a thatched house with no name' (the house in the Park known earlier as Kent's cottage, now replaced with a modern house), and thatches it himself. 'If you want to write to Harry you just put 'Henry Ellcombe, Binsted Park'. "That'll find me," he said with a grin. "Everyone knows me around here."'

So it was we finally left Binsted with happy thoughts to take us on our way; feeling just a little queer at not being, as everyone else in Binsted is, on a cycle (we saw a road worker on a tricycle), but hoping that this little Sussex village will preserve its inheritance and with its staunch 'do nothing' strike hand Binsted down to the generations yet to follow.

The Wisharts *Luke Wishart*

In the middle 1920s my grandfather, Sir Sidney Wishart, who had been city-based and Sheriff of the City of London, decided he wanted to live in the country. My grandfather had been instrumental in the forming of what was then the insurance company General Accident, initially in Perth and then in London. He moved first from Cuckfield to Hove and then purchased Church Farm, Binsted, mainly as a country residence. He was interested in farming only as a hobby and entered animals, mainly sheep, in various local and county shows where many prizes were won. Some of these prizes still hang in the garage at Church Farm. My grandfather was soon taken with country life and having been in the artillery naturally took up shooting on the farm. He appointed Mr Gatland as his keeper, who lived in a wooden bungalow in Wincher's Copse deep in the woods, known as Scotland House. Mr Gatland had a son called Jim with whom

Sir Sidney Wishart.

I went to Walberton Primary School along with other local boys from Binsted and Walberton.

During this period I spent many happy hours learning how to snare rabbit, learning how to shoot, using ferrets to catch rabbits and control vermin on the estate, as well as playing football in a team at Walberton. Summer holidays were spent building rafts on the rife and winter days tobogganing down the slope next to Binsted church. After school Fred Hotston, who worked for my father at Marsh Farm, taught me how to drive a tractor, and later Reg Tutt taught me how to drive a combine. All this was an essential introduction to my lifelong interest in and commitment to agriculture in all its forms.

My grandfather died in 1938, but before this, in 1928, my father Ernest Wishart purchased Marsh Farm and moved into the house and lived there until his death in 1987. My father was a formally educated man (Rugby and Cambridge) who was expected to go into my grandfather's insurance company. However, during his Cambridge days my father (like so many of his contemporaries) came under the influence of two causes which were to influence his whole life. One was W.H.Hudson, the naturalist writer, who introduced him through his writing to the world of nature and especially birds. This became an enduring passion. He helped form the Sussex Wildlife Trust and purchased a farm at Sidlesham bordering Pagham Harbour in order to protect the wildlife on the Harbour. This farm was sold to West Sussex County Council on his death so that the area could be protected in perpetuity.

The second influence which affected my father at Cambridge was Communism, which he took up with enthusiasm and dedication. He saw it as a philosophy which was counter to capitalism but also as a necessary opposition to Fascism which at the time was gaining a huge following in Germany, Italy and Spain. As part of this interest he set up a company, Lawrence and Wishart, and published very left-wing books. During the Spanish Civil War he did all he could to support the anti-Fascist government and later to give aid and support to the many refugees resulting from the Franco fascist government. Later during the Second World War he gave over his London house for the Czech government in exile.

My father married my mother, Lorna, when she was 16 years old. She came from a large family (7 sisters and 2 brothers), one of whom was at Cambridge with my father and introduced them. After Cambridge my father decided on a country life and purchased Marsh Farm to be near his ageing father at Church Farm. He took up farming before the War, helped by his brother-in-law, Mavin, who had worked on a farm in Argentina. Mavin was also a Communist who had been involved in the Spanish civil war on the Republican side.

My mother, largely self-taught, developed a wide circle of artistic friends through contacts in the publishing business, but also

Lorna Wishart.

the Bloomsbury set. One of her sisters, Kathleen, was the mistress and then wife of Epstein, the sculptor; another married Roy Campbell, the Catholic poet who fought for Franco in the Spanish civil war.

My mother became a Catholic in her 50s and like many converts took up the faith with tremendous zeal. It is her faith which initiated the statue next to the pond in Binsted Park. My mother had three children. Michael, the eldest, became a painter; he died in 1997 and was buried in Binsted churchyard. I was the second son and the third child was my sister Yasmin (really a half-sister, whose natural father was the poet Laurie Lee). Yasmin married a master at Dartington Hall School and lives in Devon on a farm near Totnes.

When my grandfather came to Binsted in the middle 1920s it was a rural backwater. It had no school, no shop, no mains water or drainage, no electricity. My grandfather installed a water main for the village which supplied any house wanting to be connected. This he did with the Portsmouth Water Company (still in business). There were two cars in Binsted – his own, and one other. There had been a Sunday school held in the barn next to Oakleys Cottages, but this failed to continue. My grandfather later purchased Walberton Farm and installed Bill Ingham as a tenant and manager.

During the 1960s my father, anxious to protect Binsted Woods as a whole, purchased the wood known as Binsted Wood together with land and Binsted House from Mrs Pethers (Bill's mother). Binsted Woods remain the largest block of ancient Sussex woodland south of the Downs and need protecting. They are managed under the auspices of the Sussex Wildlife Trust who advise a rather benign regime, 'Do little, save most'!

As to the village now, I regret that the family are not able to help provide low cost housing for locally born inhabitants who are unable to afford the exorbitant house prices now prevailing. This is detrimental to the forming of family roots in the area and does not help in producing village cohesion. However there are occasions like the A27 bypass campaign, the Strawberry Fair, and more lately the Millennium Book project which do a great deal to bring together all the village inhabitants. Perhaps this is enough for the inhabitants of Binsted who hold to an independent spirit. Long may it last.

Chapter 3   'The best place on earth'

Clare Druce

The journey

Pigeons strut around our feet, pecking at crumbs, cooing among themselves. We're in Victoria station, where the huge black and white clock looks down upon grimy iron railings, long wooden benches and hurrying crowds; a place of not-to-be-lost tickets and shiny stone steps down to subterranean ladies' lavatories reeking of disinfectant, where you mustn't on any account sit on the seat.

Now our mother is gazing up at the departures board, unsure which platform to head for. A clank and a clatter and suddenly the signs miraculously change. There it is, the train we want, stopping at Barnham Junction. She gathers us and our luggage together once more, and we show our tickets to the man at the barrier, hurry along the platform, climb into the train and struggle along the corridor. There's a carriage with two empty window seats! Helen and I absolutely must be by the window. Our mother puts the luggage up in the rack above us (a sort of hammock) and we settle down. Not long now.

With a jolt, a hiss of steam and a shudder we're drawing out of the station. Quite soon all we see is the backs of miles of London houses with their little garden areas. There's a woman hanging washing out; it's spring, and the sun is shining. Then we're into the suburbs, and the gardens are bigger and greener. Gradually the houses become more spaced out, and at last we're staring at proper country.

After half an hour Helen and I are getting bored, and start complaining; why couldn't we have had some chocolate for the journey? (Sweets are strictly rationed, and in short supply, but we still ask.) Seconds later a gentleman sitting nearby casually lobs a chocolate bar in our direction; our prayers answered, and so very unexpectedly! We thank him sincerely, and unwrap the present. Our mother says we're by now at least half-way there. Half-way, to absolutely the best place on earth, Mill Ball, in Binsted.

*   *   *   *   *

Secluded, two/three bedroom bungalow circa 1920 with land, in quiet hamlet. Well laid out gardens. Three large conservatories. Suit commercial grower. *So might an estate agent have described Mill Ball in Binsted, at the outbreak of World War Two.*

My sister Helen and I were evacuees, but immensely lucky ones: our mother came too. Through a friend, our parents had heard of a Mrs Malin who took lodgers. This out-of-the-way Sussex hamlet might be just the place to go, to escape the perils of the London area. Air-raids threatened our nights and days; the warning siren could begin to wail at any moment, sending us stumbling down to our dank underground shelter in the back garden. Our father, already thirty-six, had volunteered for the Army, and was soon to be abroad for three years, with no home leave.   Our mother, like so many others, was left to cope alone with small children and a war.

For our first visits to Binsted, Mrs Malin and her daughter Biddy lived alone, though amidst an ever-changing tide of life, human and otherwise; after a few years, Niels Nielsen joined the menage.   Mill Ball, this 'ordinary' bungalow, was to become our mother's beloved bolt-hole; for us children, it was paradise.

*   *   *   *   *

I listen to the rhythm of the train wheels, and try to decide whether the chunky shapes lined up along the tops of the telegraph poles are little birds; I want to believe they are, but have my doubts; I don't ask, to avoid risking disappointment.   Hedges are showing green, enclosing small Sussex fields.   Surely we must be nearly there.

At last our mother says the next station is ours, and we put our coats on and sit down again, impatient but cheerful.   Then the train slows, and we can see the big station sign, and there on the platform is Biddy, and she's caught sight of us. Amid the smell and hiss of steam we scramble out, into the sweet Sussex air, to be hugged.   There's a black taxi waiting in the station yard, and once the cheery driver has stowed our cases and bags into the space beside him we can start off.   Soon we're hemmed in by high hedges; now and again there's a five bar gate, and we can see the fields.   Our mother and Biddy are talking non-stop.

Now we're into familiar territory.   There's Beam Ends hill, and Mr Hare's cottage, then the Black Horse, the Glebe House, the little Norman church, the kissing gate into the field that slopes down to the stream full of sticklebacks; the Rectory, half-hidden

Helen in hay field.

by a massive cedar.   And in between, the simple hedges and fields.   Then at last we see the flint of Biddy's barn, standing grey and peaceful, and soon, reaching above the treetops, the metal wheel of the water pump.   Moments later we turn into the entrance to Mill Ball.

The tall gates with their peeling brown paint have been left open, and the taxi grinds slowly up the gravel path between the hazel bushes, past bright edgings of polyanthus.   In the orchard on the left we glimpse patches of wild daffodils.   Then Mrs Malin emerges round the side of the house, from the kitchen door, a small figure wiping her hands on her apron, smiling amid the confusion of seven or eight dogs all barking a welcome.   We've arrived.

Mrs Malin

Mrs Malin, small and deeply wrinkled, was perhaps not yet sixty when we first visited Mill Ball, in 1941.   A spare little figure, her head poked forwards from her collars like a tortoise's from its shell.   She seemed to work almost without pause, though once a week would take a whole day off, walking the mile or two to the main road to catch a bus into Worthing, to visit her sister.

I picture her forever at the kitchen sink, preparing the mounds of vegetables brought in from the garden; or bent over the range tending great saucepans of foul-smelling meat for the dogs (horse, I realised later).   She cooked all our meals too; I especially remember silky wild mushrooms fried for breakfast, and the rich dark taste of duck eggs, once we'd sliced through the tough turquoise-blue shells.   (Mill Ball boasted a resident goose aged thirty-two, but I don't recall goose eggs; probably Mrs Grey had given up laying decades earlier.)   Children's tea might be corn on the cob picked that afternoon, with a drink of fresh milk from 'Mrs White', the goat.   At a time of rationing and general hardship, food at Mill Ball was luxurious, with fruit, including figs, peaches and nectarines in abundance, in the summer months.   Mrs Malin was down to earth, though.   'Flavour otherwise unobtainable', she'd say firmly, if anyone found a fat cooked caterpillar amongst their cabbage.   Unenlightened in some ways, she held that brown bread was 'white bread plus the floor sweepings'.   We children were comforted when she assured us that 'fingers were made before forks'; no wonder Mill Ball mealtimes were so relaxed.

Mr Malin had dealt in wholesale vegetables in London, and the couple married in St James's church, Piccadilly.   Then they tired of the big city and bought their Binsted smallholding.   Mr Malin planted many of the trees from seed.   A statuesque monkey puzzle tree, now destroyed in a storm, stood on the lawn.   Had he once held the seed of that giant in the palm of his hand?   I suppose he set up the conservatories and greenhouses and dug the lily pond (in which I nearly drowned), or were these already in place?   A sepia photograph of Mr Malin, framed in pale walnut, hung above the sideboard in the living room; there he stood, benign and patient amid his stooks of corn.   I must have asked what happened to him, to be told he died after going out into a cold East wind.   For years I pictured him issuing forth briskly from the kitchen door, where the fig tree grew, only to meet that deadly blast.

Mrs Malin was already a widow when we first came to Mill Ball, and she and Biddy toiled alone, taking in lodgers from time to time to make ends meet.   I remember there were two elderly ladies, Miss Guinness and Miss Moore (the former part of the famous Guinness family) among others.   And the three of us.   Were we ever all there at the same time?   My memory fails me, but I do know there were ways and means of solving logistical problems in that modest bungalow.

On our visits we usually took over the two proper bedrooms, while Biddy made do with a sleeping bag spread on the living room floor (she claimed to like the arrangement, especially in winter, when the fire glowed red into the small hours).   Her mother, however, went to greater extremes.

At a little distance from the house, along a cinder path, and beyond a row of sombre conifers where the ferrets lived in cages, stood a large shed (or was it a caravan?).   Occasionally we glimpsed its interior, crammed full of items of unwanted furniture, piled high, at crazy angles, in all likelihood an interesting mixture of junk and antiques.   From the open door would waft a smell of mustiness, of old and possibly mouldy things.   To this Aladdin's cave Mrs Malin repaired every night, when space was at a premium.   Hopefully there was a comfortable and warm bed for her, in amongst the jumbled objects.

Hugs and kisses were not Mrs Malin's way, but I can picture now her warm welcomes and fond goodbyes, how she would load us up with fruit and flowers - huge bunches of gladioli, and bags of apples and plums at the end of the summer - when we must return home, to what she insisted on calling our 'pocket handkerchief' garden.

Once, Helen and I wilfully broke the rules, picking two unripe peaches, and to our horror were caught red-handed. As we hurried off with the spoils, hard and velvety-green in our hands, Mrs Malin emerged round a bend in the path leading from her nocturnal quarters. Quick-witted as any criminals, we tossed them away into the bushes, but too late.

This breach in good behaviour must be dealt with, and just that one time we were sent to bed without supper. Mrs Malin's kind heart couldn't bear the harshness of the punishment for long though, and it was she who later crept into our bedroom, with a tray of warm milk and chocolate biscuits. A week's banishment from the conservatory proved not too bad: we soon discovered that the most perfectly ripe peaches dropped through the open fanlights, onto a flower-bed below.

Biddy Malin

Biddy (christened Mary) was twenty or so when we 'found' Mill Ball, our mother Violet ten years older. The two developed an almost sisterly relationship, tragically cut short by Biddy's untimely death.

A fine posture, determined chin, an abundance of glossy chestnut hair; a young woman always dressed for a hard day's work out of doors; full of humour, generosity and tolerant down-to-earthness. Somehow, Biddy found time and space for all of us. Typically, she took the trouble to write to our father, serving abroad with the Eighth Army. How he appreciated her letters: 'Would you thank a girl friend of mine in Binsted for her letter. Tell her I was hardly 'pestered' by it. In fact, it now lies in my breast pocket, over my heart. Soon I will reply' (Italy, 17.12.1944).

Then, I saw Biddy's life through the eyes of a child. Now I'm amazed by what she achieved. In summer, peaches and nectarines cropped prolifically in the large conservatory and greenhouses, needing regular attention - pruning and tying in the branches (great dusty bunches of raffia hung from the roof for the purpose), and finally picking and despatching the fruit, to arrive at market in perfect condition. Mrs Malin looked after the poultry, goats, dogs, and probably the vegetable garden too, plus the general running of the house, so Biddy was free of all those concerns. But there were still acres of apples, plums and soft fruit to be tended and marketed, and endless watering in hot weather. One of my last memories of time spent with Biddy is of her teaching me how to make a siphon. Together we practised submerging a hose in the murky rainwater collected in one of a series of galvanised tanks near the house; edged with green slime, the contents provided a perfect gathering place for mosquitoes.

How did Biddy still find time for her flower garden? In summer the beds around the lily pond glowed with asters and gladioli, hot, bold colours, testament to green fingers and perhaps some seepage from the nearby septic tank. Biddy just loved flowers. For years our mother and she would meet up in London for a day out at the Chelsea Flower Show.

Knitting intricate Fair Isle patterns was her speciality - Helen and I wore pixie hoods, then jumpers; I remember the excitement when parcels arrived at our home in Croydon, all made in Biddy's 'spare time'.

The two 'sisters' occasionally ventured forth together to wartime dances in nearby Ford. Did they ride their bicycles in pitch darkness, in their dance frocks, in the blackout? Might there somewhere be an American airman who still remembers these two lovely young women, one so dark, one with shining chestnut hair? Before starting off, they would come to kiss Helen and me good-night, leaning over the beds smelling so deliciously of face powder and perfume; we sensed their suppressed excitement.

For a while, Biddy was engaged to be married to someone called Dick. 'Dick's sweet on Biddy', Helen and I chanted to each other, sotto voce. But the engagement was broken off.

Shortly after the war Biddy started a dairy farm with Niels Nielsen. Biddy would be up at five, to cycle along the lane for the morning milking. Helen sometimes helped in the dairy. One morning I was at last deemed old enough to go too. At sunrise Biddy and I walked across the fields from Mill Ball, just the two of us. (The only bikes available were full-size; many times I tried to ride one, standing up to pedal, always ending splayed in the ditch.) It had been a wet night, and now rays from the rising sun glanced off the meadow grasses, glinting with all the colours of the rainbow.

Standing near the pond one hot afternoon I overheard Biddy telling my mother about the lumps around her neck, the early symptoms of Hodgkin's disease. Now a form of cancer with a good hope of recovery, the outlook was bleak in the early 1950s. Despite the best treatment medicine could offer, at London's Royal Marsden hospital, she eventually lost her battle. Once, I visited Biddy in hospital, on my own, a tongue-tied teenager, but I know she was glad to see me. The last time we spoke, she was phoning from her hospital bed, her voice terribly weak. Not long before her death, she and Niels married, which made her very happy. I remember her writing to our mother, saying how she was darning his socks - a real wife. Then we had a letter from Mrs Malin, telling us how she and Niels had been at Biddy's bedside when she died.

Niels Nielsen

Niels came to live at Mill Ball just after the war. For years I fancied this tall Danish stranger had come knocking at the kitchen door one dark night, asking for work. I can see him now, standing hopefully in the doorway, just visible in the light of the oil lamp that's shining on the brass handle of the pump to the right of the doorway, where the dogs' leads hang. Now I realise his arrival was in no way unexpected; we just happened to be there on the evening he moved in, and children will jump to conclusions.

The new lodger took over the small dining room for his retreat, a room formerly put to a variety of uses: I remember it as somewhere to stow Bella or Netty, mothers to litters of spaniel puppies (one of Mrs Malin's sidelines), and boxes of musty cobnuts in autumn. Now, it would be out of bounds to children.

Niels was tall and broad, with wavy golden-red hair. I picture him

Niels Nielsen with Clare and Helen.

always in cords and an open-necked shirt, full of energy, laughing a lot, radiating fresh air and cleanliness. His English was excellent, but he spoke with a strong accent, in a surprisingly high-pitched voice. His presence amply filled a gap at the heart of Mill Ball. I suspect Mrs Malin came to look on him as a son, a most welcome man about the house. Eventually, and all too briefly, he was to become her son-in-law.

Niels and Biddy built up a dairy herd of around twenty Jersey cows. The farm was at the far end of Binsted, half a mile from Mill Ball, past the turnings to Marsh Farm and picturesque Hoe Lane Cottage (haunted, by all accounts). The gentle golden beasts all had names, and only the unpredictable Stella was not to be approached by us children. At milking time they would amble into their stalls, each to her own, to munch contentedly on the cow cakes that awaited them in small individual containers. (We children found them delicious too; they must have been highly nutritious, rich in molasses and linseed - and weevils.)

Milking was by hand, then machines were introduced. The dairy was always spotlessly clean, the channel where the cowpats fell being forever hosed down. Smelling freshly of a special bleach and of the cows' warm breath, it echoed to the clanking of metal on stone. Niels put up with us hanging around the farm with good grace - only once did he lose his temper: the fastidious Dane was beside himself with anger when he found Helen washing her feet in the sink in the dairy, near the day's cooling milk. But his fury didn't persist beyond the afternoon.

In the barn we played for hours, jumping from the highest level to the one below, landing on the dusty hay bales, smothering in prickles and the scents of high summer. Below the farm the fields stretched down to the Arun. In those days clouds of blue butterflies hovered in the summer air - we were not to know they would become endangered. Perhaps some still flutter there, but not in the same lovely profusion.

At summer mealtimes Niels was impressive, fearlessly catching wasps and squashing them between the palms of his hands - there were always plenty about once the fruit had ripened. I can picture him at this dangerous sport as we all sat around the dining table listening to 'The Archers'.

I don't know why he eventually gave up the dairy farm to concentrate on fruit farming. My mother supposed the decision was an emotional one; he'd always been reluctant to send his beloved cattle off to slaughter.

Prisoners of war, and other strangers

Gangs of Italian prisoners of war worked on the land. As a change from more back-breaking tasks, they gathered twigs from the Binsted hedgerows and wove dolls' cradles and little baskets for Helen and me; longing no doubt for their own bambini, wondering when they'd see them again.

They were emotional, these Italians; one sobbed like a child in the Mill Ball kitchen as Mrs Malin put a plaster on his cut hand. He was despised a little for his lack of stiff upper lip, but perhaps was barely out of his teens, at the end of his tether, wanting his beloved Mamma. Mrs Malin's kind heart proved enough to open the floodgates.

Paul was a tall and handsome German POW. We children liked him. Somewhere I have a photo of Helen and me standing either side of Paul, smiling amongst a field of potatoes. What were his thoughts as the camera clicked? Perhaps he'd left children of his own, maybe two little girls even, back in Nazi Germany.

Andreas the Latvian was (to me at least) a romantic figure, dark and striking. I never knew his history and now it's too late to enquire. He worked on the land at Mill Ball and at six years old I was in love with him. I didn't know till years later of his weakness for fermented beet (a by-product from a crop intended for the cows); how he'd be found sprawled on the path, hopelessly drunk on the illicit brew. Suddenly he left for Wales, to be a coal miner, which broke my heart at the time.

Left to right; Biddy Malin with Violet and Helen.

Mill Ball in our time

On some of our visits Helen and I share Mill Ball's double bed. It's in the first room on the left as you come in at the front door; Mr and Mrs Malin must have slept there, in the old days. Now it's night, and I'm staring into the darkness with my eyes wide open, trying to make out where the window must be. But I can't tell. There's no moon, and because we're deep in the country and everyone must observe the blackout, there are no lights showing for miles around. But I'm not scared. The feather bed is cosy, and Helen's there beside me, with her cold feet (mine always warm up first). We never need a nightlight, after the candle's blown out.

What accounts for the musty and delightful smell of this room? It must be the mixture of feather mattress and old-fashioned furniture, dust, the scent of apples stored in the loft overhead, all mixed up with the sweetness of the damp air from the open window.

There's a big Victorian wardrobe, a marble-topped washstand with pitcher and bowl, and a tall old chest-of-drawers. One window looks onto the drive and the hazel trees beyond. From the other window, on the wall I'd been gazing at in the darkness, you see the box hedge and the quince tree, then the big lawn. The windows are low; you feel you could quite easily climb out, and the box smells strongly spicy when the sun beats down on it.

The other bedroom, the next along the hall, has single beds and just one window, looking onto the drive. This is the room heated in winter by the Valor stove, because we feel the cold more, sleeping separately. Perhaps it really is the coolest room in the house, because it's where Sally, our special dog, chose to creep under a bed years later, when she was feeling the heat badly in her old age. Memories of furniture here are dim - certainly it was dark and old.

In the kitchen, the sink is under the window and we can just see Mrs Malin washing up, if we pass by in the garden. On the left, as you come in from the hall, there's a cream-coloured Rayburn, saucepans steaming and rattling on top. To the right stands a long and cluttered sideboard. Toby the cat often sits hunched up on there. Old and bony, he is given to sneezing, but is well away from any food. Once dusk falls, all too early in winter, oil lamps and candles light Mrs Malin's way.

But there's no scullery, no laundry room, and I don't think about washdays. Did the outhouse behind where the peaches grew, opposite the back door, hold a sink and a mangle? Water must have been heated to warm the conservatory, and perhaps served both purposes. Such practicalities didn't concern me, not for one moment.

The bathroom is full of interest. A marble-topped table holds endless bottles and items of Biddy's makeup. The bath is cast-iron, a little rusty, with friendly-looking claws for feet. In spring, it might be completely filled with bunches of the delicate wild daffodils that grow under the apple trees. The combination of the piercingly sweet aroma of the flowers combined with TCP is a heady one. The intention every year is to take a good quantity of daffodils to market, but sometimes gypsies get to the orchard first, then it's they who make the sales. Next to the bathroom is the lavatory, with no frills. Mrs Malin, generally so tolerant, demands that we children are less extravagant with the toilet paper. There are few strictures at Mill Ball, and we're a little taken aback by this.

The living-room is where everyone gathers. It's quite large, with windows on two aspects. One looks into the conservatory, and Mrs Malin uses her treadle Singer sewing machine beneath it, where she can catch the best light. The sofa stands where the other windows form a square bay that takes up all of the south side of the room, looking onto the lawn and the monkey puzzle tree, whose glossy spiked branches rise high into the air, defying close examination. From the left angle of the bay you could see over to the pond and the greenhouses, and the brilliant flower garden. Helen and I often sit here if we're waiting to go out, or just to be around our mother and Biddy as they chat. If you thump the cushions, clouds of dust rise up, to catch in your throat. Next to the sewing-machine there's the sideboard, more modern than the bedroom furniture; it's in a pale, golden coloured wood, walnut perhaps. There stands the large battery-operated wireless, crackling with wartime drama, later to relay the joys and sorrows of 'The Archers', fictional but liberally spiked with solid information for farmers. Newspapers and magazines clutter the rest of the surface.

On the opposite wall there's a brick cottage-style fireplace where a fire burns in winter. A collection of Toby jugs grins down at us from the mantelpiece, in descending sizes. To the left of the fire a range of shelves hold the household's books, mainly agricultural and horticultural volumes, no doubt essential to Mr Malin as he planned his orchards and first trained the young peaches and nectarines onto their stout wires.

Next to the bookcase is the piano, pretty and old-fashioned. I'm fascinated by the little wooden weather house on top. The woman comes out in fine weather, the man if it's going to rain. Beside it stands a framed embroidered picture of Victorian ladies skating on a frozen lake, their hands warm inside muffs as they glide along in their long skirts. On the other side of the doorway there's a tall glass-fronted cabinet. The living room door is permanently propped open with a door-stop in the form of an elephant's foot; perhaps it's real.

The middle of the room is taken up by a round mahogany table, the surface protected by a chenille cloth of indeterminate colour. It's supported on three central legs with sturdy polished claws, and surrounded by a set of plain and solid Victorian chairs. In the centre of the table there's an oil lamp. All our meals are taken round this table.

The carpet is a worn cotton one; its faded blues and oranges are echoed in the loose covers and cushions of the sofa, and in the colours painted on the Toby jugs. This is a bright sitting-room, where on fine days dogs are to be found relaxing on the floor in patches of sunshine.

The front door is always open in the daytime, so we often come and go this way, through the dry and dusty conservatory filled with plants. A plumbago has been trained onto the wall beside the door.   Several feet tall now, its trunk gnarled, it's covered in a mass of delicate blue flowers in summer.

The entrance hall feels important.   A mirror, pock-marked with age, fills the whole of the wall at the far end, dimly providing extra light by day, reflecting the flicker of candles after dark.   Heavy Victorian or Edwardian furniture lines the wall, on the living-room side.   A grandfather clock stands to the right of the door, its face richly decorated with paintings of the sun and moon.   There's a long dark cupboard, with patterns carved into the wood and display shelves above.   These hold an array of interesting ornaments, the silver ones tarnished to the colour of bronze.   I especially appreciate a little silver bear.   The fur of his coat is finely etched, his tiny eyes seem to look right at me, and his hinged head may be carefully opened and closed.

Before electricity

Imagine the glow of candles and oil lights, friendly pools of brightness among shadows. Remember the bedroom on cold winter nights warmed by a Valor heater; how we lie sinking into soft feather mattresses, the air thick with the comforting smell of paraffin.   Above us, a golden pattern from the decorative design on the heater's top imprints itself on the ceiling; it's magic, and I want to hold onto it, for ever.

Mrs Malin perches each evening on her high stool with its dented seat of tan American cloth, brief moments of relaxation with the newspaper.   After dark she reads by the light of a tall oil lamp at the centre of the round mahogany dining table, while the rest of the room retreats into darkness.

There's no television of course, and the battery-operated wireless is mainly switched on to catch up with the news, all important in wartime.   What we hear is conversation, dogs barking, perhaps 'Prossy' pushing a squeaky carpet sweeper around, hopelessly battling with dust and dogs' hairs.   (Mrs Prosser cycles in from Walberton regularly, to 'do' for the Malins, bringing them news from the outside world.)   I like to pick out tunes on the old piano, though Mrs Malin does once ask me to stop.   On this occasion my few bars from the Funeral March, repeated ad nauseam, are too mournful to be endured for a moment longer.

Half a century later we arrange candle-lit dinners; we like a softer, more flattering environment, just for a few hours.   Having no choice in the matter makes for different attitudes.   When electricity finally came to Mill Ball, around 1950, Mrs Malin didn't bother with fripperies like shades.   Bare bulbs gave out even more of this modern wonder, available at the flick of a switch.   And so Mill Ball was changed for ever, the gentle illumination of candles and oil lamps traded in for the glare of a bleaker world.

School days and games

Sometimes we attended school in Walberton, where Captain and Mrs Taylor ran Red House School.   We would walk with our mother over the fields; she stayed with us for the day, helping in some way.   Often we ran into a group of children heading the same way.   In winter one little girl was always crying pitifully.   'She's cold', her peers explained to us, when our mother showed concern.   In summer, we nibbled on ears of wheat, plucked from the cornfield that edged the footpath.   They tasted sweet and creamy; how deeply depressing to think that today toxic chemicals might be sprayed on the crop.

Memories of this stage in my education are dim.   I can see Captain Taylor, wearing his permanent black eye patch, pointing with a ruler at a large map of the world pinned up on a *blackboard. And I fancy he taught us about different species of birds. I remember the daily neck exercises (probably excellent ones) insisted on by Mrs Taylor. 'Yes - No - Of course not' we chanted, the last bit involving a full rotation of the head. Beyond that, nothing, except vague impressions of pleasant rooms. I'm sure we spent one night in the Red House (was it too snowy to get home across the fields?) and picture the three of us sharing a pretty attic bedroom.*

Shop bought toys played no part in our lives, in the long spans of time we spent at Binsted. Penelope and Tessa Dendy of Glebe House were our special friends, and together we roamed the lanes and woods, inventing games and adventures. Parents didn't fear for their children's safety in those days, as they must today. As Mrs Malin said, any stranger would be noticed immediately, and cars were a rarity.

I remember the four of us conducting funerals, the deceased being small figures cut

The pond at Mill Ball.

out of perished inner bicycle tubes; we buried them with ceremony in a patch of dry and dusty soil beside the peach conservatory. Once we crept into a deserted cottage in the fields behind Mill Ball and came upon a weird relic - a rock-hard bun, left behind in the rusty, long-abandoned kitchen range.

Sometimes we played 'dares', and I was the one chosen to go up the spooky overgrown path to 'Old Dicky Denyer's' to ask for a drink of water. Eventually a rather severe old lady opened the door (a housekeeper?), and reluctantly shuffled off into the forbidding recesses of the house, to oblige this strange child. The well water tasted queer, which served me right. Years later I could hardly reconcile what I remembered as a dark and gloomy 'cottage' with the elegant eighteenth-century 'Meadow Lodge' that came to light once the overhanging bushes and trees had been cleared.

Under the green canopy of a weeping willow in the garden of the Glebe House we talked and argued happily. Noisy play near the house was not allowed, as our friends' step-father worked from home - Mr Bryceson was 'Hotspur', the Daily Telegraph's sports correspondent. If we forgot ourselves, the window of his study would burst open, whereupon we soon quietened down.

Once or twice we went to Marsh Farm to visit Yasmin, a cousin of the Dendy sisters, and, as is now widely known, Laurie Lee's daughter. Vague impressions come to me of high grey stone walls and the spread of an ancient mulberry tree. Yasmin's mother, Lorna Wishart, was a striking beauty, sometimes to be seen cantering through the Binsted lanes on horseback. (I picture her in a flowing cloak.) She joined the Church of Rome, and erected a shrine to the Virgin Mary at a pond in Binsted Woods. Rumour had it she put a string of real pearls round the Virgin's neck. Rumour also had it that a farm hand stole them, which perhaps was not to be wondered at. Yasmin's brother Michael was to become an artist of note; we saw some of his earliest work - murals painted on the attic walls at Marsh Farm. Much later, we girls realised that Yasmin's other brother, Luke, was a handsome youth. One warm summer's evening, as mists rose from the meadows by the church, we stalked him, Penelope, Tessa, Helen and I. Although dusk was falling, the white sweater Luke was wearing kept him in our sights till it was almost dark. Was he aware of having four admirers?

Though doubtless planted out by Mr Malin to be coppiced, the trees in the copse had become overgrown. Hazels entwined their branches overhead, while shallow streams bridged by logs meandered along in the shady world below. Criss-crossing each other, they gleamed among pale primroses and wood anemones that carpeted the ground in springtime. For hours we'd lie on our stomachs watching darting sticklebacks, and the spindly water-boatmen who travelled the water's surface.

The large pond lured us too, and once nearly proved fatal to me; on our first visit I'd plunged in, a reckless toddler after a lost peach. By the time Helen had alerted the grown-ups, nothing but my summer bonnet could be seen, floating idly on the surface. However, I was soon spotted, but was fast turning blue when fished out by a soldier who happened to be visiting. He apparently showed great presence of mind, and inverted me, allowing great quantities of murky pond water to be evacuated. For a few days after that my mother slept uneasy in her bed, with the knowledge that a dead rat had been noticed in the pond the previous day.

Years later, Helen and I decided to wade across the same pond. Tucking our frocks into our knickers, we lowered ourselves gingerly into the thigh-high water. The disgusting sensation of rotting vegetation and what felt like bloated drowned worms between our toes ensured that we never did it again. Once more, the goldfish who swam lazily under the sheltering lily pads could live undisturbed.

Somewhere near the poultry house was a large shallow pit, into which broken crockery and other non-combustibles had been dropped over the years. This made a fertile ground for investigation and discoveries. Scallop shells were there in abundance for some reason, and these made useful tools.

Christmas presents were strictly limited. A child today might say 'Is that all?' on unwrapping the last one of dozens of gifts. I remember the second of the two Christmases we spent at Mill Ball, and my two presents. One a brown bear (possibly home-made), the other a kaleidoscope, three-sided and covered in black mottled papery material. Inside this dull exterior was a world of magically shifting patterns, in the brilliant colours of a brightly-lit stained glass window. One flick of the wrist, and everything fell into yet another wonderfully symmetrical arrangement. I wish I'd kept it, and the friendly brown bear.

I believe that Christmas was the white one. I can picture standing at the back of a crowded Binsted church singing carols, while the snow lay round about, deep and crisp and even. It was probably the year I was outraged at being considered too young to join the children tobogganing down the steep hill beside the church.

Ladybird was a one-eyed ex-polo pony, on whom I sat aloft occasionally, held tightly by Biddy. For company Ladybird had Silver, an aptly named horse; together they lived peaceably in the fields between Mill Ball and the barn. On an earlier Christmas, sadly not remembered by me, Biddy and our mother dressed up (one presumably as Father Christmas) and drove the pony and trap up the drive past our bedroom window, bells a-jingling.

Sally was a golden retriever. She grew greatly attached to our mother, and became looked on as 'our' dog.   Brought to the Malins by her London owner on a temporary basis, she was never collected.   Mill Ball dogs (nine of them at one count) were not taken for walks, being free to roam the acres of land at will.   But clearly Sally had laid down early memories of the delights of properly organised outings.   A lead was superfluous in the quiet lanes, but for propriety's sake she'd carry one, folded in her jaws, to proceed a little ahead of us with her ladylike walk, turning to check that all was well if we lagged behind.   Sometimes we'd tie her up outside the church, where she'd wait patiently - we children went inside quite often, to play a few notes on the harmonium and climb up into the pulpit, or just to look around; it was never locked.   We loved the simplicity of the whitewashed walls, the feeling of age.   Our Sally, so dignified and devoted, became a touchstone among dogs.   We loved all the Mill Ball dogs, from Gillie the Great Dane, through assorted spaniels, down to Mrs Malin's adored toy poodle Mandy ('no bigger than a jam jar when I first got her'), but Sally was our special friend.   With her steady character plus a West London background, she could surely have starred in 'Peter Pan'.

The wind sighing in the telegraph wires; soft Sussex rain making puddles to splash in. Electric-blue dragon-flies, bodies fat as a man's thumb, skimming the water-lilies, on brilliant gauzy wings.   A toad, throat pulsating, eyeing me guardedly from the safety of the pond's overflow pipe (only visible to one willing to lie quite flat and peer awkwardly under the rim of a sun-baked flagstone).   The rustle of the breeze in a clump of bamboos.   The pungent scent of the box hedge under the bedroom window.   Hard, sweet-smelling fruit from the quince tree, so gorgeous in spring, growing near the front door.   Huge 'puffballs' appearing overnight on the lawn, to be kicked around.   Plums, apples, raspberries, peaches, nectarines; animals in abundance.   A kid-goat newly-born to 'Mrs White' carried into our bedroom first thing in the morning, to be admired; adults who loved us.   All this, and friends to mess around with.   What more could two children want?

Postscript

For some thirty years I was out of touch with Niels.   Then one cold March day in 1985 my husband and I were driving with our daughter Emily through Sussex; why not adapt our route a little, and call in at Mill Ball?   As we drew up outside the familiar, tall wooden gates the plan suddenly seemed foolish.   Would everything be different, would my memories be spoiled for ever?   Would Niels still be there, even?   Oh come on, they said, now we've come out of our way...So we walked up the drive, and nervously I knocked at the kitchen door. After what felt like a long wait, it was opened by a stranger.   No, Mr Nielsen did not live there any more.   Well, of course!   All that time had passed, thirty years or so, I should have known...

We were turning away, apologetic, when the unknown woman added 'But you'll find him outside somewhere, pruning the apple trees'.   We soon discovered our informant was Jane Hollowood, Binsted resident and a scriptwriter for Eastenders - she was working in the hoped-for peace of the now uninhabited Mill Ball.   Cheered, we went back down the drive and into the orchard, to where the wild daffodils used to grow under the old-fashioned fruit trees (replaced now by modern commercially-viable varieties, planted in straight rows).

We see a figure at some distance, anorak hood up against a biting wind.   When we get close I feel I must check that this distinguished-looking elderly man is indeed 'my' Niels, before I reintroduce myself.   He pushes back his hood and says yes, he is indeed Mr Niels Nielsen. But who are we?   The reaction when he realised that I was the Clare of 'Helen and Clare' was infinitely heart-warming.

'No! Helen and Clare!' became his delighted refrain for the next hour or two. Coffee was suggested and we went indoors. Understandably, he found it hard to reconcile this forty-something woman with the child he'd known. Emily provided a much better reminder, and he instantly warmed to her. We sat around the familiar round dining table while he explained he was living at Beam Ends cottage, but still working Mill Ball's land. Even now he seemed to be trying to keep the house and garden as it had once been, replacing plants that had died with identical ones - a new plumbago of the same delicate blue flourished in the conservatory, by the little-used front door.

Sadly, many familiar ornaments were missing; there had been burglaries in our quiet, safe Binsted; times had changed. A whole drawer was missing from the sideboard - thieves had taken it, complete with the silver, and the Toby jugs had gone. The kitchen was just somewhere to make a cup of coffee, the range long since cold. Yet the spirit of the place was strangely and most comfortingly intact. Someone had brought in a branch of peach blossom from the conservatory, to brighten the living room. There it stood, in airy simplicity, unaccountably vibrant with the old Mill Ball magic.

The next time I returned, Helen was with me, and we met with the same warm (you could say rapturous) welcome from our living link with the past. It was no mistake, this coming back together. She too knew instantly it was still 'our' Mill Ball - the place where as children we knew, in advance of every visit, that we would be quite extraordinarily happy.

The last time we saw Niels we visited him in Beam Ends cottage. There with him, for safe keeping, was the old Mill Ball grandfather clock, its face painted with the moon and stars. Now he was not well, said he was getting old. He'd seen a ghost, a friendly one, evidently, since it had thought to tuck a tartan rug around his knees as he sat in his chair. Not long afterwards Jane wrote to tell me Niels had died. She said many people had come to his funeral to mourn his passing, and that his ashes had been scattered around Mill Ball's lily pond.

Mill Ball: further notes *Bob and Joy Davies*

When we first knew Mill Ball in the 1980s and subsequently made our home here in 1992 much was still as Clare described. The archway of hazel from gate to house helped to foster the feeling of peace and seclusion. The woodland is a seasonal delight of daffodils, bluebells, orchids and primroses. Following major coppicing there was an abundance of magnificent foxgloves over 6ft. tall. The lake in the woods is a peaceful retreat. Both woodland and lake are home to a variety of wildlife – much returning year after year. The orchard of apples, pear and plum trees is still productive, keeping us busy most times of the year and providing food for a variety of wildlife.

Delving into old paperwork we found that in 1923 Herbert William Malin purchased a total of 26 acres of land from Sidney H.F. Upton of Marsh Farm. In addition in 1927 he purchased Mill Ball field, with the flint barn, from Charles Ernest Read of Manor House, Binsted. In 1924 Mill Ball bungalow was constructed, by a local Walberton builder, A. Booker, for a total cost of £885. Water came from a well close to the kitchen and in 1936 the installation of a wind pump enabled water to be piped into a holding tank in the loft – a labour-saving device. The pipe-work was still in evidence in 1992.

Following the death of Herbert Malin on 1 March 1939 his widow, Hilda (Ellen

Rebecca) passed ownership of Mill Ball to her daughter Mary, known as Biddy, in 1949. Biddy married Niels Nielsen and after her death in 1954 Mrs Malin continued to live at Mill Ball with Niels. A memorial stone in the woodland commemorates Niels's life (24 May 1911-28 March 1990).

Other interesting discoveries we made include the wooden peach boxes, complete with their padded inserts, large egg crates, tin cans and the equipment for canning, and Mrs Malin's treadle sewing machine. Today, despite the modern comforts of central heating and fitted carpets, much of Mill Ball still evokes memories and shows evidence of its former years. To our family and visitors, it offers a peaceful haven from general 21st-century life. We feel nothing could be more appropriate than the description in Clare's title, and consider ourselves very fortunate to have our home here.

Chapter 4   Wartime and after

The pub in wartime

Bill Pethers, born in the Black Horse pub at Binsted in 1940, remembers it as another safe haven. 'They bombed Ford and everybody was frightened for their lives. We all congregated over at the Black Horse.   Goodness knows why, because we had a shelter at the back of the house. I have vague memories of going down into it.   Dad said we only spent about three nights in there, and basically the water table came up and we were up to our knees in water in the morning, so they abandoned that.   They thought it best if everybody congregated in one place, and there seemed to be less chance of dying. At the Black Horse it was warm, it was light - we had no electricity at the Manor House. It was all oil lamps - we did not get electricity at home until about 1950.

'I can remember being taken across the Park.   Obviously we did not go along the road, we came along the back beside Kent's Cottage, and Dad had a big old bike.   He built a piece of wood on the crossbar and I sat on this lump of wood, with my feet on little straps in front - it was not very comfortable, I can remember that - and he would cycle across there.   Mother could not ride a bike, and I can remember her trailing along behind.   We would all go across there every night and come back early in the morning to see to the chickens, geese and dogs.   It was only at night time that we actually left the place.   In those days you could leave a house, even in the middle of a war, and you would not worry about burglars, you were worried about the Germans bombing you in the night.

'None of our bedrooms at home were heated.   It was bitterly cold and they used to say that as a baby, I would scream the place down when I was over here, and as soon as I was taken across to the Black Horse I immediately stopped.   In fact they got into the habit of putting me in the carrycot and would bang on the door, 'here he is', and bang, they would leave me there.   Nan would scoop me up and it was always warm and comfortable over there, and there was the smell of - I don't know, cigarette smoke and beer and voices, and everything seemed to be happy.

'The Black Horse in those days, even after the war, was the centre of the village really. Everything went on there. People came to the Black Horse

The Black Horse pub before it was rebuilt in the 1920s.

from all over the country. Nan and Grandad were there for forty odd years so she knew everybody. Nan was the centre of attraction, she ran everything. She brought all these evacuees down in the war. I mean, you could bring one or two down, but she brought about fourteen. They were living out there in the hut - a large wooden building that was converted, warm in the summer and freezing in the winter. All the money from the pub went on food for people and it was more or less frittered away. The evacuees went on coming down here, years later they were bringing their grandchildren. She would always put them up, there was always a bed somewhere. All the rooms upstairs were given colours; I was born in the Yellow Room, facing over the back. There was a Pink Room, a Blue Room, and all these rooms were painted their colour. She had these great big feather beds, you know the song 'Grandma's Old Feather Bed' - they were like that. You had to scramble up on top of this thing. And the wind used to howl, I can remember that, because it is very exposed. There was no double glazing and the wind used to whistle through the windows.

'During the war, I can just remember, you could not go to sleep at night because of the noise, singing and shouting and dancing outside. Every day seemed to be a party. Grandad was a real Cockney lad. He was brought up in the East End and he had all these songs - he could reel off rhyme after rhyme after rhyme, song after song. The piano used to be played and people were singing outside; buckets of beer - because they couldn't get to the bar, you'd serve them with a bucket, they'd go and help themselves.

'At the Black Horse during the war my recollection is of troops being there, people in every sort of uniform. We had some New Zealanders, and a lot of RAF people. There was Danny Daniels, I think he was a Pilot Officer by the number of pips on his shoulder. He was killed, and a lot of the pilots that visited the pub, they were gone. Out of six of them, four of them died. There were stories that they used to tell, Auntie Rene said they ran out of beer at the pub and they would go off down to Tangmere or down to Ford and get invited into the mess where they had some beer.

'The place was always full of smoke. When I was old enough to serve at the bar, about 12, in the evening the smoke would come down and down like a smog, and you could see this sort of gap where the people were. The ceilings were low, and it just seemed to build and build, until you could only just see people out of the gloom.'

Nan and Grandad Pethers

Bill's grandmother, Winifred Pethers, had a particular reason for mothering him. 'I was the only grandson - the only grandchild. Uncle Jim, Dad's brother, had lost twins, I think, when he first got married, and to compensate Nan lived for me. There were always pictures of me everywhere - it was almost to the point of embarrassment, particularly in a pub. I lived at the pub when I first got married - I was nineteen and had a young family, and in the navy they didn't give you houses then. Sitting there drinking your beer and there was Nan saying 'Billy, come and pick some flowers for so-and-so', and I'd say 'No, I'm twenty-five years old!'

'Nan was a business woman, there was no doubt about that, but whenever she made money she just gave it away again. She always had a present for me of some description. She never spent anything on herself. She ran the Women's Institute in Walberton, and she used to organise plays and pantomimes and trips all over the place. They'd get a charabanc to Oxford, or to Lyme Regis on the coast, and it was good for

Harry and Win Pethers.

business as well. She very rarely got a lift anywhere, she'd always walk to the bus to go shopping. She had an old pram which she'd leave up at Beam Ends, and when she came back from Sainsbury's or Bognor she'd have five shopping bags in her hands - the strength some people have - and stagger down the road to where she'd left the pram, and load it up to bring home.

'Nan was always the last to lock up, and this is gone midnight, or one o' clock. She'd do the books, and one thing and another, and she was up at five o'clock in the morning. I never saw her sit down and eat a meal at the table. She served everybody, and she would sort of pick at food - she would be seen nibbling, but I never saw her sit down and eat. The only time I saw her eat anything was when we went down to, say, Littlehampton, to the fish and chip shop, and she would sit down and eat fish and chips - that was very rarely. Otherwise all she'd do was cups of tea and nibbling dry biscuits.

'Grandad was always puffing on his pipe, always changing his tobacco, banged it out on the table, all over the place. I got on well with my grandfather, he was a very interesting man. You would not think he would end up as a Binsted publican. When he lived in London he was one of the first electrician journeymen. He worked for the Gas Board, all the Pethers did, in the East End of London - if you were a Pethers, you got a job. He built lovely radios - I've got one of his radios, built in 1921, I think it is. It had brass on it, and he was good with his hands. He had a small lathe. But apart from that, he was always interested in what went on in the world. If somebody invented something, he was onto it, and he had this club in London where working men would pay so much and get some famous man such as H.G.Wells to come and talk to them, and Grandad would introduce the speaker. He was a workman and he always had an inquiring mind.'

Henry and Margaret Pethers

Harry and Winifred Pethers' son, Henry, worked as a gardener for Charles Read of the Manor House until Mr Read died in 1939. 'You can see from the pictures that it was beautifully maintained. It must have been part-time, because he worked at Toynbee's nursery in Barnham full-time. He was very friendly with my Grandfather [Mr Read]. He was fifteen years younger than my mother [Margaret Ernestine, the Reads' daughter], and the main thing that brought them together was their great love of dogs. They both loved the country, they loved the peace and quiet, and they both loved books - from different angles, Dad was more a Somerset Maugham man, and Mother was more Warwick Deeping, but they both loved Dickens. Anyway, they obviously found a mutual interest, and I think a mutual dislike of my grandmother [Florence Read], who had become quite bitter. She had decided about 1935 that she would go to bed and

Margaret Pethers, daughter of Florence Lewis and Charles Ernest Read.

stay there. Doctors came and there was not anything really wrong with her. This is the vicar's daughter, and she always considered that she had married below her station. Poor old Grandad, according to Dad he was a lovely old man, a typical country gentleman.

'I think my father took pity on my mother, and she wanted somebody to console her. Right from the word go she had been treated like a doll; she was not allowed to go out playing, and there were only certain people she was allowed out with. People would come and visit, but she was not allowed to go to school because she was too delicate, and she had governesses - good education but a terrible start in life really. She was not allowed to mix with other children and Mother dearly loved to talk to people - she would talk for hours about the family. Though there was a mismatch in age she and my father obviously thought a lot of each other, and eventually married in secret. Wally Valance, who owned the paper shop in Walberton, was best man and they had a special licence and were married in Chichester. Then, of course, they had to keep it secret from my grandmother. They lived in the same house [Manor House] with her upstairs and them downstairs.

'Of course, 'the lady' as she was called, when 'the lady' found out there was all hell let loose and off she went - she booked herself into a nursing home. I mean, this was not some little old lady, she was a tyrant. She had the money, and she hired a suite of rooms in this nursing home and off she went. The funny thing was, apparently Mum and Dad were sat in the kitchen having their breakfast at the table and there was a bang on the door and a furniture lorry had come to collect Mrs Read's furniture and that was the lot. She took all the furniture out. They could not do anything about it, it was her furniture. So they literally put their breakfast things on a box in the corner - she even took the table they were eating off.

'I did meet my grandmother. I called her 'Granny Worthing'. I don't think my grandmother really approved of me. There were some little trinkets addressed to 'Billy', but I don't remember any pats on the head or cuddles.

'I think after I was born, because of the difference in age Dad and Mum became further and further apart. There weren't any major rows or anything like that, but it was in some ways a very cold atmosphere. Dad would go off to the Black Horse to see his parents, and Mum would be stuck here with me, and of course, as I got older and started to go out, she would be stuck here on her own. I went off into the Navy and then there was my sister, who was four years younger. Again, a girl in this sort of place, she wants to get out and see the bright lights.

'Dad was very particular about his food. He would never eat chicken, he would never eat pork, turkey he would not eat, lamb he would not eat - he would only eat beef, ham and bacon.   Nan used to give him exactly what he wanted.   She used to come across and do the cooking to start with.   After every dinner, he would have to have something with custard on, and only his mother could make custard.   So he had to go and get her so she could make the custard.   This must have been very embarrassing for my mother.   He used to go round to the Black Horse every night, about seven, half past seven, and he would have one pint of beer and that would be it.   He would sit and drink that all evening.   They always had supper, bread and cheese every night, and then he'd come home, about eleven I suppose.

'My Dad was a very good chess player, and a very good card player too.   He played cribbage.   He was very friendly with Charlie Baker, the gamekeeper. They would go round the Black Horse and play, and in those days there wouldn't be the queues of cars you see out there now, in winter time, basically, the pub closed down.   They would all gather round there on a Friday evening and play cards until two or three in the morning, and the beer carried on pouring.

'Before my Dad died he told me that he didn't think his mother and Grandad got on very well.   He said 'That woman, what she did to my father', and there were tears running down his face.   He said he led a dog's life, Grandad Pethers, and apparently she had been a real tyrant to him.   So that's two grandmothers who were tyrants.'

Henry Pethers in 1986 with Jet.

Games and gangs

'My earliest memories are of being pushed in the pram up the plantation, towards Baker's (Pinewoods now).   My mother used to take me up there nearly every day to walk.   In those days there were not all those conifers there, there were beeches and mixed trees - very picturesque.   During the war I had this little pedal car, Dad had made a wheel out of wood - you could not get toy wheels and glass and all those sorts of things - and I used to hurtle up and down in this thing, and slam into the bottom of the end of the path and straight into the step.

'We went to Walberton school.   We'd all meet on what we call 'Hotston's corner', next to Grove Lodge, and the taxi used to come and pick us up.   It is pretty remote down here for a child, but once I'd been to school and met up with other people, we used to go down to Climping swimming from school, on our bikes.   We'd go through Yapton - now Yapton was a terrible place.   The Yapton oiks would be chucking bricks at you and of course, you'd go all the way down swimming and the little blighters would be waiting for us when we came back.

'At school you either came in shoes or boots, and that's hobnail boots.   You were definitely at a disadvantage with shoes, because boots really hurt when you got kicked. But you soldiered on - you either talked your way out of it or gave as good as you got.

In Walberton there were always little gangs of people. You would come round the street corner and there would be X, Y or Z gang and they would be after you - a bit like the Yapton lot but not quite so vicious!

'When I was older I had several chums in the village. We were all little horrors. Dad's favourite saying was the Chinese saying, 'Even the stones in the road dislike a boy of 9 or 10'! There were bits in the paper about us - 'We know who you are'. We were today's vandals I suppose.

'I was thrown out of the scouts in Arundel - up to some mischief. I used to cycle; Dad gave me a bike, a Rudge Whitworth. On the main crank of the pedal there was a hand. Everyone else had bright shiny bikes, but Dad had painted mine with aluminium paint. He'd read up somewhere that it would reflect heat and he painted anything that did not move. We used to pedal off down Hospital Hill, hurtle down there, hit the bottom, and get thrown off. We used to roller-skate and play roller hockey. We got ourselves some shinty sticks and used to play at Beam Ends and on the Yapton Road. Then the school took pity on us, Avisford Park school. One of the masters came down in his car and nearly had one of us. He said we'd got to get off the road, and we said we had nowhere to go, and they allowed us to go up into the playground of the school because the boys then were on holiday.

'Then we found the delights of Brighton. I was getting on a bit then, I was about ten. We used to go to ice hockey in Brighton on the train. We would pull all the light bulbs out, throw the cushions out the windows, fuse all the lights, the police would chase us…happy old days. Some of the boys actually stood outside while the train was moving. They would dare each other to get out of the carriage and stand on the side.'

Farming memories

'I can remember driving tractors out here with Freddy Hotston. I was only about eight or nine then [1948], and tractors were a lot smaller than they are now. Both fields were put to corn, and while they were throwing the stooks up on to the truck, I learnt how to drive the tractor. I couldn't reach the pedals, but I could go along, and I could reach the brake. In another couple of years I could reach the pedals, and one day when old Mr Wishart was having a big demonstration of a new baling machine, with farmers who had come up from all around the area, I drove around the field in front of all these people, which was quite something.

'I would be out there in the boiling sun, and I'd have trousers with braces, and when you'd take the braces off there'd be white stripes where I'd been burnt. There was a big silage pit there too, and they used to put molasses in big tanks. Once I fell into the molasses tank. It wasn't very high, but it was like falling into black syrup.

'The molasses was to put in the silage pit. They would start with a pit, very deep, about the depth of this room, then build it up with layers of hay, molasses and chalk or something, until it was a mound equally high and you could walk on it. Then they would come along with huge hand cutters, slice it and dig it out and feed it to the cattle.. It retained the goodness, added value to the hay.

'There were snakes all over the place, grass snakes and adders. They loved the silage pit because of the warmth. It was great catching snakes because the snakes would come out of one hole, see somebody there - and snakes can't reverse, can they? And they'd pop into another and then you'd find half way along there would be the snake, and you

Fred Hotston on a tractor with Terry.

could pull it out. It was usually grass snakes that we caught.

'The silage did smell, a very sweet smell. As you come through the gateway, that's where it was. It was in the house and everywhere, and of course, we were downwind from it. There were cows on the Park and all around the old house, wandering all over the place. They used to drink out of the pond. They were Mr [Ernest] Wishart's cows; we let the big field and Broad Green to Mr Wishart before he bought them in the 1960s. Years ago, this was all sheep country, they used to close the gates top and bottom and that's why they had the haha, to stop the sheep getting into the house.

'The farm which is now Bee Bee Kennels was bought after the war in 1948 by an ex-RAF officer named Bowley, who ran a turkey farm. He had a manager there called Scott, and I used to play with his daughter, Sheila. Niels had the barn next door, and he had built this silage pit - well, not a pit, it was up on walls, and we kids had gone round through the barn, like kids do, and we were in our welly boots and thought it would be a good idea to walk all over this silage pit, and of course he followed our footprints. When we moved back here, Niels seemed just a little old man, but in those days he was quite a hefty chap. I remember we just stood there and this giant of a man came up and said 'Who's been on the silage?' We all denied it and out came his hand and he hit me so hard he nearly knocked my head off. I can still feel that club to the side of my head - there were stars, I was almost semi-conscious for a while. I was really wary of the man after that.

'Bowley of Binsted' went bust - it didn't help that local lads came and stole all the turkeys. The whole of that area was bought by the Kallis, a Greek Cypriot family, mother, father and four children. They owned a restaurant on the front at Bognor, and ran their place here as a pig farm, and all the residue from the restaurant they used to feed to the pigs. They were a very generous family, but the boys had to work, and if you were up there playing with them, you had to work too, carrying those big oil drums that took about five gallons, one on each side of a yoke you put on your shoulders.

Each side was filled with pig swill, and you'd flounder through the mud, and when you pulled one side up, the other side would go down.

"The Kallis had all sorts of machinery up there with the farms and how we did not get killed, I do not know. We were playing with motors and everything. There was electrical stuff and water everywhere. The pigs were dangerous as well. You would go in there to feed them, and you'd get in there with a sow and a big litter, and she'd really have a go and you'd have to jump out very, very quickly.'

Niels and farming *John Hosking*

Niels had come to England from Denmark as a young man in 1939 for a year, to study English farming methods. Due to the outbreak of war, he was unable to return home at the end of his year. John Hosking, of East Harting Farm, writes:

Niels had applied to the Danish Embassy to find a suitable farm, and my parents were selected, here at East Harting Farm. Having little English, Niels spent his evenings (before television) with the newspaper and a dictionary. But even after many years in England, part of his great attraction was his deliberate misuse of the language. He would speak of 'smouldy' breadcrumbs in the making of Danish Blue cheese.

I first met Niels when I was ten years old, and knew him as 'Nugs'. He was extremely strong, having spent his student holidays as a navvy on Danish Railways, and he could carry sacks of wheat (two and a quarter hundredweight) from the thrashing machine up the steps to the granary, and keep this up all day. He would pitch sheaves of corn until the wagon was loaded well above the ladders, and was not content until he had a real load.

Niels was one of several students at East Harting Farm, but he showed an entrepreneurial flair. He asked my father for a couple of acres to grow corn (maize) cobs at a time when the Americans were over here prior to D-Day. In the autumn of 1943 Messrs Poupart of Covent Garden took all he could pick at the then huge price of 1/- a cob. The following year, he decided to grow onions: a year that turned out to be a shortge year for onions.

At the end of the war Niels decided to farm on his own account. Small farms locally were difficult to find, but Messrs Stride of Chichester were offering 20 acres with a good set of buildings at Binsted. The flinty soil was off-putting to Niels, but my parents (who offered help with finance) pointed out that the flints would hold the warmth at night. He was persuaded, and my father's diary for 1946 records 'Lorry left with Niels' - presumably with some animals as well. As there was no dwelling on his land, he stayed at Mrs Malin's half a mile away - a kindly soul, who provided a home from home. He rented more land, and had a very successful herd of Jerseys. The amount of concentrate (cattle cake) that he used horrified my father, who was brought up in more austere times. Later he established an orchard for his 'retirement', also a success. Niels left many friends at Harting.

Haymaking *Clifford Blakey*

A Laurie-Lee-like note is struck by a memory of pre-war farming from Clifford Blakey, of Havenwood Park in Binsted parish. As a boy, he was often sent to stay with his mother's parents, who were tenant farmers in Hertfordshire. 'Most memorable of all was fetching the hay harvest in. We children 'helped' (?) in the fields, or got in everybody's way. The last wagon-load heaped up like a mountain on the wagon pulled by a tired old horse at the end of the day. We kids climbed on top into a soft nest of sweet-smelling hay where we clung to each other in fear as the wagon rocked its way out of the field. We were flung together by the action of the cart and sun-burnt limbs, thin summer dresses and golden hair were mine to enjoy as we rode home.'

Land girls *Jean Hotston*

Jean Ranford came to Binsted as a land girl in 1943, aged 19, to work in the cow stalls at Marsh Farm along with Cyril Thomas, the cowman, and Arthur Blackman. It was here that Jean met Fred Hotston. Fred was the son of a family that had been in Binsted for generations. His father, Alf, the foreman, was born at Marsh Farm and joined the forces in World War One, moving back to Binsted when Fred was four years old. Also working on the farm at that time were three other land girls, Mr Blackman senior and Dan Bolton who worked with Nobby, an old shire horse used for carting.

Cart with straw bales, with the Collins brothers (carters).

Jean and Fred were keen photographers, and their photographs record many scenes around Marsh Farm including its thatched barn and 'round house', where a horse once went round and round in order to work machinery in another barn. This small round building on the north side of the barn was later given by Ernest Wishart to the Weald and Downland Museum at Singleton which still has it in store.

Thatched barn at Marsh Farm.

Jean recalls how Fred picked up a young rook in the drive to Marsh Farm when it fell out of a tree. She writes: 'It was called Joey and became very tame but caused quite a commotion in the village at times. It would fly up the lane where people had washing on the line and pull out the clothes pegs. It was a great torment to gardeners. Jack Pearson at Grove Cottage kept a broom by the back door to chase it away because it would pull out his shallots as soon as his back was turned. Fred's mother had two cats. They loved to sit in the sun on the garden wall at Grove Lodge. Joey would hop along the wall until he got near enough

The thatched 'round house' at Marsh Farm. A horse walking round inside it worked machinery in another barn.

to peck their tails and then quickly fly away.

'The Co-op used to deliver 'Lord Woolton' pies once a week in the morning to Grove Lodge and Fred's mother would cycle round the village to deliver them. She would hide the door key under a pot and one day she returned to find it wasn't there. She guessed Jocy had taken it as he watched her hunting for it with his head cocked to one side. She had to go to the

Mrs Lily Hotston (Fred's mother), Joey the rook, and Bob (father of Terry).

farm and get Fred to come and break in. Once she was indoors Joey looked at her and dropped the key on the doormat.

'Ruth and Stella, who lived in Walberton, used to cycle out from Valences' paper shop to deliver papers and confectionery. They would leave their bikes propped up outside Grove Lodge and Joey would pinch things out of their baskets. Once he flew off with a packet of cigarettes and they dropped out one after another like a string of bombs.

'Joey was firmly installed before I was billeted at Grove Lodge and he didn't like me. He used to perch at night on a shelf in the scullery and if I went near he would cry "Go away" and flap his wings. He would also mimic cats and would sit in the trees in the drive to Marsh Farm and many a time people would say "There must be a cat trapped in a tree". It would be Joey.

Rene Shaw and Joan Jefferies, land girls, about to load hay, with Jean on top of the rick.

'One day Fred's mother and sister Doris cycled to Barnham to catch a train and go shopping in Portsmouth. Joey followed them and as the train left the station they saw him flying around. They never saw him again. A good while later a rook appeared at the open window of the scullery at Grove Lodge and kept putting twigs on the windowsill as if building a nest, but we could never be certain that it was Joey.'

After the war Jean and Fred married and after living in Slindon settled in Binsted in 1952 in 'The Screens', the house they built in the field of that name. Fred died in 1979, aged 54, and Jean stayed on until 1985. Fred loved wildlife; his nature notes about Binsted were often published in the Parish Magazine which covered both Binsted and Walberton.

'The fox in Binsted' *Fred Hotston*

It was 3 o'clock in the afternoon of a day in early March. Above the brooks near Ford station, a number of rooks were behaving in a very strange manner. They were swooping down out of sight behind a clump of blackthorn bushes, then climbing and swooping again a little further along. A few seconds later, past the end of the bushes, a slinking animal appeared. The objective of the rooks was revealed as a fox. Keeping close in to the low hedge which divided two fields he moved cautiously forward with his brush held low. Now and again he would pause, glance up at the rooks, peer over his shoulder and then advance again. In a few moments his quarry appeared, prancing around merrily. Two March hares. They saw the fox; became motionless; and as the hunter grew near, they flattened themselves to the ground. Then followed a most amazing sight. The fox began to circle round the hares, getting closer with every turn and the hares too got up and began to circle round as well. Suddenly the fox stiffened, sat on his haunches, put his nose in the air, and loped away, apparently having scented the presence of a human being.

Binsted in the 1940s *Nell Hornak*

It was a hot summer's evening in 1942 when my mother, my sister Tessa and I arrived at Ford Station. I was about six or seven years old at the time, Tessa three years younger, and despite the war we were filled with a sense of adventure. We were off to the country to stay with the Wisharts, who were distant relations of ours. Lorna Wishart and her son Luke and daughter Yasmin met us at the station pushing a pram. We put Tessa in it and started our long walk back along the road, through Binsted woods to our temporary home at Glebe House. The sun was going down and the leaves made a dappled pattern across the uneven track lining our route.

We lived at Glebe House with the Wisharts for a short time. We then stayed in the annexe of Beam Ends for four or five months before moving to Morley's Croft at the far end of the village. It was a magical time for children used to town life...with the exception of the winters. We had no electricity at Morley's Croft, oil lamps for lighting, a paraffin stove for cooking and water was pumped from a well in the garden. Tessa and I had to take it in turns each morning to perform this odious task. There was a water gauge in the bathroom and one of us had to stand by and wait until it read 'Full' before yelling to the pumper to stop before we were discharged from this duty. It was jolly hard work for two small girls but it had to be done.

With no heating in the cottage except for a log fire in the sitting room, winters were miserable. I used to stand facing the fire and get roasted in front while the back of me froze.

The walls ran with condensation and the sofas were always damp. We hated the cold. Tessa and I had countless childblains on our fingers and toes, which were agony. Mummy used to knit mittens for us which helped a little. At night we used old stone ginger beer containers filled with hot water as makeshift hot water bottles to try to keep our feet warm, but both were literally stone cold by morning. We huddled together for warmth.

Mummy had a little Ford car that was kept in a shed at the bottom of the hill. At night during the long cold winter months we had to light a lantern, put it under the car and cover the bonnet with a thick army blanket. Surprisingly enough this was not always successful and often my mother had to crank the car to start it.

In the beautiful Georgian house opposite (Meadow Lodge) lived an elderly brother and sister, Mr and Miss Denyer, and their maid Sibby. She often came across to look after us as a sort of babysitter, and to help Mummy in the cottage. Sibby fascinated me. She looked like a tiny elf. She was about 4ft 6ins tall with little round glasses and brown sandals that curled up at the toe. In the house she always had on a floral apron, but her best and only outdoor clothes were a brown tweedy coat with a velvet collar and a large-brimmed brown felt hat. She clutched a bright pink plastic-looking envelope handbag which didn't quite match the rest of the outfit! She wore this attire every Sunday to church. She was always telling us that she had a boyfriend who used to pick her up on his motorbike, and she used to 'read' the newspaper upside down. We never saw the boyfriend or asked her to read to us from the paper. We adored Sibby.

For a treat Mr and Miss Denyer invited us over to the house to watch them make butter in their cellar. It was very dark and dank down there and quite frightening for us small children. In the middle of one room stood an enormous contraption with a handle which was turned for what seemed like hours, until the creamy milk suddenly changed into a large lump of butter. We thought it was magic! Mr Denyer had two Guernsey house cows, Buttercup and Daisy.

At the age of nine I was sent to boarding school and only returned to Binsted in the holidays. By this time we had moved from Morley's Croft to Glebe House and it was at this time that Tessa and I met Helen and Clare Spalding who were evacuees from London. We had wonderful times with them inventing all sorts of games and having all kinds of adventures. Our favourite was a trip to the haunted house…the ruins of Binsted Manor. At this stage only the roof was missing from the house, and we would climb the rickety stairs to the first floor and examine various broken pots and pieces of china that to us seemed like priceless treasure. There were a few chairs about the place and a broken down grand piano that was half-way through the floor. There were stairs to the cellar which were rotten, and we dared each other to go down to what looked like the bowels of the earth, little appreciating the dangers of such a mission.

Tessa and I had been forbidden to go there as the whole area was by now considered quite dangerous. Driven by the possibility of finding something exciting in the cellar we carefully picked our way through the rubble towards the blackness dislodging some old masonry as we went. This created a mini-landslide and we all came out covered with brick dust and rubble. There was serious trouble ahead for us as a result of our expedition and we were grounded for several weeks.

We ambled along the lane as children without a care in the world. Tessa, being that much younger, was sometimes a source of irritation to me. It was with great delight that I was able to negotiate a deal with the cowman's daughter next door …her doll in exchange for

Tessa and her pram!   My memories of Binsted as a child were of long hot summer days, freezing cold winters with hard frosts and snow, and a glorious sense of freedom.   Despite the war these were carefree days for us children, spent wandering about the countryside secure in the knowledge that we lived in a safe and caring community.

The Misses Denyer at Meadow Lodge.

Chapter 5   Air crashes in Binsted

There were so many air crashes in or near Binsted during and shortly after World War Two, due to our closeness to the airfields at Ford (Royal Naval Air Service) and Tangmere (Royal Air Force), that they almost became a matter of routine, at any rate to local reporters.   Not, however, to the inhabitants, especially small boys.

Air crash at Binsted Park, 1952   *Bill Pethers*

It was 13 May 1952.   As usual, I had returned from Walberton School and was having my dinner with my grandparents at the pub around 5 pm.   I was tucking into some ice-cream, when we heard the fire engines going by with bells ringing (no wailing sirens then).   There was a knock on the front door, which Nan answered, and I could hear 'Jumbo' Blunden (my chum who lived nearby) shouting 'Was I there?'   A plane had crashed on my house (Manor House) and to 'Hurry up because everyone was heading off to the scene in the Park'.   The ice-cream was forgotten, and I was off down the road pedalling like mad, not knowing what sight would meet me when I reached what was left of my home, knowing my parents and sister were there.   As I reached the top of our hill I was relieved to see our home and my family safe.   There was, however, a giant plume of grey smoke coming from behind the trees next to the pond.

Following an engine 'flameout' and the safe ejection by the Royal Naval pilot, a Supermarine Attacker jet fighter from RNAS Ford had crashed part in the field and part into our copse north of Binsted pond.   The fighter had dived into the edge of the copse behind the old pond garden, leaving a very large hole in the field.   The fuselage had completely disappeared into the flaming cauldron of the hole it had made, and a lot of wreckage from the wings and tail had literally been blown into the copse.   Parts of the trees had been burnt and whole hazel clumps torn out from their roots and strewn about, as though a giant had kicked them out of the ground.   There were large clods of earth and foliage all over the field and down in the woods in the lower pond.   The smoke I had seen was coming from this big hole in the ground.

About 12 feet in diameter, the deep hole contained a glowing white powdery mass of metal that tended to burst into flames at the slightest breeze.   This 'flare-up' was immediately attacked with hand-held foam fire extinguishers by the Naval ratings standing by the smoking hole.   Our local fire crews, however, soon lost interest in the event and were busy rolling up their hoses (I don't think water was the best medium for fighting an aircraft fire and it would most likely have caused another explosion).   We small boys and the Naval fire crew were left standing around sorting through the bits and squirting foam at the small volcano in Mr Luckin's field.   After an hour or so it got a bit boring, and we boys found some sport in calling the crew from their cups of tea in the nearby RN blue 'Tilley' van by announcing that their 'cauldron' was flaring up again - they would rush over and give the fire yet another squirt of foam!   There were very few warnings to us of 'Not too close now, sonny' from the fire crew, apart from initially not letting us get too near the hole or touch the wreckage! However, there were no white tapes or notices erected, so we boys were soon stuffing our pockets with anything useful that could be swapped at school.   Unfortunately the much-prized guns and ammunition were not to be found.   One oddity was that just in front of the hole lay what was left of the cockpit surround for the canopy after the pilot had ejected.   I assume the metal had been sheared off in the impact, but it looked almost untouched.   Most of the sizeable wreckage of the wing sections and undercarriage had been blown into the lower pond garden and remained there for some days.   This gave us lads a chance to haul away and hide some of the bigger chunks.

From memory, the excitement of the evening concluded when it became dark.   The Fleet Air Arm fire crew and us lads packed up for the day and went home ready for a more exhaustive search of the site in daylight.   There was also some time to make a study of our souvenirs, with most of us hoping we had found something highly dangerous or better still explosive!   I hid some of my spoils, including a large chunk of the hydraulics that dripped pink fluid everywhere, and an inspection hatch plate (that I still have) in the stinging nettles beside our garage.   (With my Dad's help, I think, the dustmen eventually took the bigger bits away.)

What I didn't know at the time was that my young sister Gloria, whilst standing by our front gate, had witnessed the full event of the crash.   She had seen the pilot eject and float down on his parachute, and the aircraft dive behind the trees.   She said there was a tremendous bang on impact, which shook the ground, and huge clods of earth, wreckage and small trees were thrown into the air above the tree line.   Gloria still has vivid memories of the event after all these years, not surprising really as the impact occurred only 300 yards from her.   On reflection I think we all had a lucky escape.   Somewhere, however, I have a small clipping from the local paper announcing that another Naval Fighter had bitten the dust in Binsted woods, but I doubt if the reporter even bothered to make his way to the scene.   Such was the regular occurrence in those days of air accidents at the RNAS Ford and RAF Tangmere airfields.

My Anorak bit!

The Supermarine Attacker was a very unsophisticated jet aircraft for its time.   In fact the RAF rejected it because of its poor performance but the Navy used 145 of them and Pakistan had another 36.   The aircraft's wings were originally designed for the last and unsuccessful version of the Spitfire, called a 'Spiteful', with a new fuselage containing a single Rolls Royce Nene 3 engine.   The engine was to be used successfully later in its two-engine mode in the

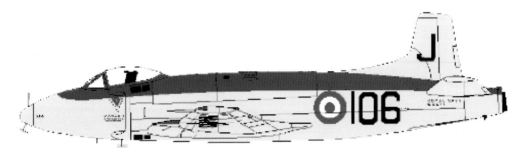

Supermarine Attacker WA493 (call sign 106/J) courtesy of Rick Kent.

'Sea Venom'. Another peculiarity of the Attacker was that the aircraft retained a tail wheel undercarriage (which must have made it 'exciting' to control on take off!) Its fully laden weight was 7870 kg, and I guess that in old money, nearly 4.5 tons of fuselage and engine disappeared into that hole in Binsted at several hundred mph - no wonder there was such a 'big bang' on impact!

Postscript

Since writing this piece, I have rescued the inspection hatch plate I have kept in various loft spaces over the years and shown my trophy to my work colleague, Tony Wright. Tony served in the Fleet Air Arm as an airframe and engines engineer, and was therefore well qualified to reveal its secrets (if any). Tony's first observation was that the number WA493 painted on the plate rear was the identification mark of the aircraft. He recommended looking it up on the Internet (Now, why didn't I think of that?). Somewhat humbled, I searched the 'Net' and found the number listed under the Fauconberg Aerographics Aircraft Catalogue web site. The catalogue listed a Mark 1 version of the Naval Fighter aircraft as follows: 'Attacker F.1, WA493 "106/J", 800 Squadron FAA, HMS Eagle

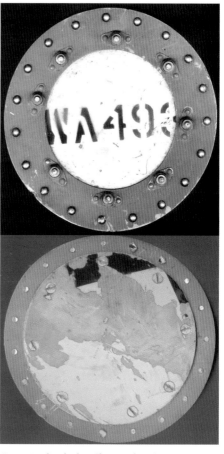

Inspection hatch plate (front and rear).

1952. One more click of the mouse revealed an excellent colour profile by Rick Kent of the aircraft, call sign 'J106'. I find this coincidence quite remarkable, because of the 181 aircraft of this mark produced, the catalogue listed only one. This happened to be the fighter that crashed at Binsted all those years ago.

I can only assume that the stricken aircraft was a) attached to 890 Squadron and based at RNAS Ford, or b) flying with 800 Squadron from HMS Eagle and using Ford as a 'diversionary airfield'. I would also like to think that the pilot who survived that day went on to reach happy retirement. Who knows, he may read this and wish to toast his good fortune?

Martin Sutton of Walberton adds: 'It would seem that 890 Squadron was formed on 30 January 1952 at Ford with the purpose of acting as a pool of pilots and aircraft for both 800 and 803 Squadrons.' Luke Wishart confirms the difficulty of flying Attackers. 'I flew with the Fleet Air Arm during my National Service and sometimes at Ford. The Attacker was a horrible plane to fly, and was quickly replaced. This crash was due, I believe, to what is technically called 'flame out'; this engine was prone to doing this after large throttle movements at slow speed, e.g. in the landing circuit. This made it quite a handful for inexperienced pilots like us.'

Mid-air collision, 1955

On 3 March 1955, Meteor F8 WE963 from 34 Squadron, flown by Pilot Officer Timothy John Hartnoll, aged 22, of the RAF, took off from RAF Tangmere but almost immediately collided with a Royal Navy Sea Vampire, T22 XG765, flown by Sub-Lieutenant B. Carter, aged 20, from RNAS Ford, which was coming in to land. The Sea Vampire flew on slightly, then crashed in woodland near the old Chichester Road (A27), close to the pub near the B2132 turn-off, now Oaks. The Meteor crashed in woodland near the Havenwood Mobile Home Park. Both pilots were killed in the crash. The Meteor pilot was buried at Tangmere.

The circuits of the two airfields were very close and instructions were issued subsequently preventing Tangmere aircraft from turning right after take-off unless absolutely essential. Some of these details come from Martin Sutton, who also writes: 'If you take the footpath just to the east of the entrance into Havenwood Caravan Site and walk south along it, you will go under the overhead power cables. A short distance further on the left of the path (when looking south) you will find a large green water-filled hole. This is the location of the Meteor crash site (Paine's Wood)'. Luke Wishart adds: 'The Sea Vampire from Ford crashed into the northern section of Barn's Copse, against the ancient earthworks, about 150 yards from the A27. An oak tree there still carries scars of this crash, having lost a limb. Other sections fell into the copse just south of Scotland Lane, where the lane enters the woods at the western end.'

A relative of the Vampire pilot, Tim Davies (the pilot was his wife's uncle), was researching the crash in 1994, with an appeal for information printed in the West Sussex Gazette. Clifford Blakey of Havenwood answered the appeal and with the help of staff at Littlehampton Museum found that an account of the crash had appeared in the Littlehampton Gazette of 4 March 1955. It quoted an eye-witness, Mrs A. Watts of the Beam Ends Café, Binsted, who told a reporter: 'I was in the garden and hearing aircraft I looked up into the sky just as two planes crashed in mid-air. They plunged down and I heard a great bang. At the same time there was a sheet of flame from the direction of some woods. It was terrible. My husband telephoned the police and fire brigade.' According to the paper the Littlehampton and Arundel fire brigades were called out, as well as rescue teams from Ford and Tangmere, but 'the woods were so dense that some rescuers lost their bearings and had difficulty in finding the crashed aircraft. The fuselage of the Meteor was still on fire when it was reached and firemen cut down surrounding brushwood to prevent flames from spreading.'

Danny Daniels, a Battle of Britain pilot who used to drink at the Black Horse. He was killed near the end of the War trying to nudge (with his own aircraft) a V1 Doodlebug out of the sky.

Mr Davies wrote 'The Fleet Air Arm Museum sent me some details of the Board of Inquiry, which established that the accident was caused by the Meteor pilot. Both pilots were young and this was a surprisingly common occurrence. Many pilots were tragically lost in accidents during this era.' Luke Wishart adds, 'The comments on the high accident rates during this era I can confirm. Among the 28 pilots on the course I started on, five had died before the course ended. Mainly this was due to the introduction of jet aircraft to young inexperienced pilots. Jet aircraft required the very rapid assimilation of new techniques, and quick reactions. There was little room for mistakes, and any made usually resulted in fatalities, or serious accidents.' Bill Pethers agrees: 'Approximately 1 in every 6 military pilots died in crashes in the early jet fighter era. The death rate was probably higher in the Royal Navy.'

He remembers visiting the site of one of the crashed aircraft 'in Scotland woods some weeks afterwards. All that remained was small pieces of wreckage and a burnt orange life raft in the trees. I also remember finding a shoe and a small yellow hand pump. The excitement I had previously felt as a young boy (I was now 14) at such incidents was not forthcoming on this occasion, although with one's chums I think we all put on a brave face. The three of us were quite shaken by the sight and smell of devastation around us. I never went back there again.'

The Canadian airmen, 1943

A crash which killed four Canadian airmen is now commemorated by a plaque in Binsted Church. It reads: 'In memory of Sgt. D. Montgomery RCAF, Sgt. W. Mackay RCAF, Sgt. J.D. Scott RCAF and Sgt. J.W. Whipple (of the Royal Canadian Air Force), who were killed on April 3rd 1943, when a Hampden Bomber (L4084) crashed on a 'Fighter Affiliation' training flight in the Parish of Binsted. The airmen are buried side-by-side in the military training section of Arun Cemetery. This plaque is erected by the Friends of Binsted Church with help from the Museum of D-Day Aviation at Shoreham Airport to commemorate the crash. April 2000.' Mr Sutton adds that it was from 415 Squadron, and dived into the ground from 2000 feet at 1050 hours and burnt out. Ken Rimell of Shoreham D-Day Museum explains that 'the Hampden was on a fighter affiliation exercise with a Typhoon from nearby Ford. Fighter affiliation exercises involve a number of friendly aircraft 'playing' at shooting each other down. In this case the Hampden almost collided with the Typhoon and in taking evasive action it entered a terminal spin and crashed, killing its crew. The Typhoon pilot was never traced.' According to him, the bomber exploded on impact, and only fragments were ever found. The site is given as near Marsh Farm. Luke Wishart adds: 'I believe this bomber fell into a small paddock behind Goose Green.'

Other air crashes

Ken Rimell points out that 'nearly all the wartime crash reports, be they AFS, NFS or police, are now kept sealed at the Sussex Police HQ at Lewes, to stop would-be aviation archaeologists from searching and digging up crashed aircraft.' Information on the other crashes in Binsted is fragmentary. Rene Baker mentioned several when interviewed by her nephew, Bill Pethers.

Mr Wadder. He crashed very close to the Black Horse, before World War Two (1936 or 7). 'He was an hotelier and territorial army captain from Worthing. He was flying a private plane that crashed at the back of the pub. Grandad [Harry Pethers] knew Mr

Wadder because his territorial units used to use the land around (and in) the pub for their exercises – well, they would, wouldn't they? Harry went down the field and clambered through all the mud and water of the rife to get to the plane. It left a great hole in the hillside.' She and Bill think Mr Wadder either died at the scene or shortly afterwards from his injuries. No documentary trace of Mr Wadder's crash has been found.

Mr Myers. Martin Sutton gives the following account, culled from old newspapers, of another crash near the time.

On Monday 17 February 1936 a 25-year-old man, Edward Myers, son of Mr and Mrs M. Myers of the Clarence Inn, Portslade, decided to hire an aircraft from the South Coast Flying Club at Shoreham and take his friend, 25-year-old Miss Ruby Dickerson, for a flight. They were going to fly either to Brooklands or Portsmouth and have lunch. Mr Myers held an "A" certificate, had around 20 hours solo flying experience and was regarded as a capable flyer.

They took off from Shoreham in a De Havilland DH. 60G Gipsy Moth aircraft, registration G-AADA, at around 12.15 pm and flew to Portsmouth where they had lunch at the airport. On their return they got airborne in brilliant sunshine but suddenly ran into a bank of thick fog. Mr Myers flew the aircraft around for some 30 minutes trying to find their way. Mr Alfred Hudson [probably Alf Hotston], a farm foreman from Church Farm, Binsted, said that he was working on top of a straw rick when, at around 2.00 pm, he saw an aircraft flying low. It came close to some houses but rose as it approached farm buildings. At the time the air was thick with fog and he did not see it again but heard it crash about 200 yards from where he was working, in the centre of a field near Beam Ends. Mr George Pelling, a nurseryman at Walberton, was near some cottages opposite the field when the aircraft crashed. He thought it was trying to land as it struck the ground almost flat. When the aircraft hit, it turned a complete somersault.

Miss Dickerson died soon after help arrived. Mr Myers was released from the aircraft and taken to hospital, and recalled the details of the flight to his brother, but died (due to multiple injuries and shock) at 4.20 am on Tuesday morning.

A German plane in the field opposite the pub. Bill remembers; 'You go opposite the Black Horse through the gate, beside Church Farm, and there were two big elm trees on a bank, and right beside them was part of the wreckage of a WW2 plane (around 1948-1950). I assume the wreckage was all that was left from the two aircraft that collided over the pub during the war.' Mr Sutton suggests: 'The nearest German loss to this location was on the night of 24/25 March 1944 when a Junkers Ju 88 was shot down. The bomber broke up in the air and the main wreckage fell near Eastergate Lane, just to the west of Walberton. Did parts fall into the field near the Black Horse as it crashed?'

A possible German, or American, plane near Scotland Lane. Rene remembers a plane crash 'in the woods near Scotland Lane where it comes out in the Park. They found legs and bodies and years after they found bits and pieces'. Mr Sutton suggests this could be an American B24 Liberator from the 489 Bomb Group, which crashed at Park Farm, near Arundel. (Scotland Lane does come out of the woods near there, near the A27.) He writes, 'The B24 had been hit by flak whilst over Normandy but continued to fly on and reached the English coast where most of the crew bailed out. The Captain (1st Lt William B. Montgomery) and his co-pilot remained on board and the aircraft eventually dived, almost vertically, into the ground at Park Farm, Arundel. Both pilots were killed. The site was fully exposed in 1974.'

A possible plane crash in the woods behind Fox's Lodges, during the War, in which several crewmen were killed.

A crash in the field behind Grove Lodge. 'There was that lady pilot flying a Spitfire or a Hurricane and it crashed in the field behind Grove Lodge. It was a brand new plane and she was bringing it in to Ford or somewhere and it came in low and crashed.' Mr Sutton identifies this as 'a Spitfire being brought in to replace some of those lost during the invasion, and the accident happened on 9 June 1944. The Ferry Pool Pilot, Warrant Officer Ernest Reginald Rasmussen Royal Australian Air Force, aged 24, was killed.' He adds that this does not tie up with the report that it was a lady pilot! Luke Wishart pinpoints the location: 'This Spitfire fell at great speed into the field 'Bedfords' north-west of Grove Lodge, and buried itself about 20 feet down. I am sure about this location as I was there within the hour! The Pilot was believed to have suffered oxygen starvation, as the plane went into the ground almost vertical. I have (or had) various pieces from this place. Unhappily, my mother threw them out when I left home.'

A crash near Goose Green. Bill remembers 'a big indent in the ground behind the house, this I thought was a bomb crater, but it may well have been the result of an air crash, as I doubt if the house would have survived a bomb going off so close to it.' Luke Wishart believes this was caused by the Canadian bomber which crashed in 1943.

Chapter 6   Recent memories

The pub and the Mayor

Arthur Wickstead lived at the pub from 1948, then in Church Farm bungalows, and now lives in Arundel.   Interviewed by Vicki Bryceson, he remembers that at the pub 'There was hardly anybody from 'outside', except on a Saturday night 'though you'd always find the odd one or two from villages round about'.   'All these farm workers, nursery workers and agricultural workers were the same sort of people, and they got on well together.'   When the turkey farm started 'round in the bottom end of Binsted', there was 'an influx of people from all over the place working down there and they used to more or less keep the pub going.   They was up there, well, every night I expect.   There must have been at least a dozen or more, and all heavy drinkers.'

Arthur Wickstead at the Black Horse.

Weekend shooting parties also helped keep the pub going.   Mrs Pethers did not sell 'anything much in food then' – as appears elsewhere, she preferred to give it away - but she did make her own pickled eggs and shallots.   The 'local bobby on a bike' had to check that pubs were observing closing time, and Arthur remembers 'one night I was in there, and a sergeant copper and a policeman came in, and "whose beer is that" and "whose beer is that", and of course, one of them was mine.   The sergeant done all the spouting and of course Henry [Pethers] said, well, I am the son from down the road and I always stop for a bit of supper last thing.   All of a sudden the copper said to the sergeant who we were.   He said I was a lodger there and someone else was a lodger there and there was his son and the old man.   The sergeant turned to the copper and said "Why didn't you tell me these people were living here?" and he said "Well you never asked me".

'The 'local bobby' was 'pretty friendly, like they were.   They could always go to the back door for a bit of information that you pick up in pubs.   Me being a bit of a pub crawler you used to get to know all these things.   Even in the Norfolk Hotel in Arundel there was always a little 'down below' bar there where the local coppers used to get together and have a 'pow wow'.'

The pub-crawling lifestyle did not, it seems, affect Arthur's health.   'I used to do a lot of cycling purely for sport then, and very often I used to get home from work, have

Reg Tutt and John North at the Black Horse in the 1960s.

my food, a proper meal at about six o'clock in the evening, and cycle off to Brighton and back, calling quite often at the greyhound racing. I had a good racing bike then. I used to do it pretty quick, but it used to take longer coming back because I used to call at about three or four pubs. Those were the days!'

John North describes the Black Horse in the 1960s and the start of the egregious office of Mayor of Binsted.

Harry Pethers was landlord of the Black Horse from 1928 until 1968. He died in 1968 at the age of 82. His wife 'Win' carried on as landlady until her death in 1969. The pub in those days was just a beer house, but Harry obtained a spirit licence before his death.

Both Harry and Win were generous to extremes. Whenever one of the regulars had a birthday, Win would supply a wonderful buffet, and wouldn't dream of taking payment. She did this kind of thing all the time that she was landlady. There were not many regulars in those days but everybody was friendly and joined in everything. Arthur Wickstead and Herbie Hampton lived at the pub, and of course were two of the regulars, as well as Reg Tutt and myself, and some of the farmworkers of the village. There was a very friendly atmosphere all round, and occasionally Harry would get up a sing-song – always the old tunes such as 'Daisy, Daisy' and other old Music Hall songs. Reg Tutt knew some wonderful old country songs which he would sing and everybody would join in.

Commander Cammidge lived in the village at Morley's Croft and became a regular with his wife. He decided that there should be a Mayor of Binsted and set things in action. Harry was our first Mayor and was made so on his birthday, Nov. 4th, 1965, and each successive year a new one was elected. It was all light-hearted and great fun, and each mayor was given his responsibilities which he was expected to carry out. Incidentally, no-one outside Binsted was chosen: it was essential that a Binsted resident be elected.

During my year in office I had rather a hard task. We had a hard winter and the snow was very deep, and I was expected to clear the roads and see that everybody in the village was not in trouble. I did my best!! I had a tough time, but we muddled through, and again I must stress that everything was done in a light-hearted manner.

It was a sad day when Win Pethers died. She and Harry had been there for so many years and were greatly loved and respected. But life had to go on. We had a succession of landlords and landladies afterwards, the pub was made bigger and a most pleasant restaurant added. People now come from far and wide to eat and of course to drink.

A footnote to the fact that the pub was 'just a beer house' in the 1960s came from Maxine Monk, who with her husband Richard ran the pub very successfully between 1994 and 2001: 'The reason was that the landowners, through the Magistrates, would not allow spirit licences because they didn't want the serfs to be able to drink what they could.' Bill Pethers adds that the cost of the licence to the landlord, versus the likely returns from a largely beer-swilling population, was uneconomical.

The Mayoral office was an occasion for much inventive satire and the BBC even came to the pub to record something about it for its morning programme on the Home Service. Several 'scrolls' from the Mayoral ceremonies still exist, as does the Mayoral chain, made of suitable materials such as miniature bottles and cocktail sticks. The scroll for 1966 reads:

LIST YE, ALL YE GOOD CITIZENS OF BINSTED REGIS.

Be it known throughout the Fair Burgh of Binsted-Regis-by-Rife, that the Ratepayers, Taxpayers, Tithepayers and Evaders thereof, have met cautiously and nocturnally with intent to Elect, Choose, Pick or otherwise select a Brother Miscreant into whose clutching hands it will be safe to entrust the Perks, Arisings, Leavings and other Proceeds of their Local Misappropriations, in the sure knowledge that he will be under surveillance day and night whilst in possession of such Misbegotten Valuables.

The Selection of such a Man for the Post also carries with it the covering Office of Lord Mayor of Binsted Regis. GOD SAVE THE QUEEN.

The Noble Office of Lord Mayor of Binsted Regis is, of course, of considerable antiquity and it should be noted that, so far, no Occupant of the Office has yet failed to display the requisite qualities of Backsliding, Crookedness, Double-Dealing and, in fact, all those forms of Nefariosity which are so necessary in the holding of any present-day Public Office if the Occupant wants to stay out of Clink.

Now, therefore, let it be proclaimed to the Burghers, Residents, Inmates and Layabouts of Binsted Regis that it seemed consistent with their Safety and Wellbeing, to appoint HARRY JOSHUA PETHERS the Jovial Boniface of the Black Horse Inn, Binsted Regis, to undertake a second Term of Office as His

The investiture of John North as Mayor of Binsted. Left to right: Reg Tutt, Peggy North, John North, John North junior, Margaret North and Henry Pethers.

Washup, the Lord Mayor of the said Binsted Regis. This we have done in the Firm Belief that he will continue further to elaborate and even to embroider, details of his previous Curious Criminal Career, and to keep in Mind wot the Burghers have been up to recently in their more crooked Bleck Deeds.   HURRAH FOR HARRY.   GOD SAVE THE QUEEN.

Given under our Hand this 1st: Day of November 1966,

Sir Bill Bogus, First Baron Backsliding of Binsted Regis. Lady 'Slippery' Pinch, Kommandant of the Ladies Kleptomaniacs Korps. Alf 'All, Just a Burgher.   Willy Washout, The Water Board.

Rene and the Bakers

Rene Baker, daughter of Harry and Winifred Pethers, married Fred Baker, one of the nine children of Charles Baker, a game-keeper for the Duke of Norfolk.   Interviewed by Bill Pethers, Rene remembered 'Fred's Dad when he worked for the Estate.   He always had a beautiful green corduroy suit – he had a new one every year, with gaiters.'

Rose and Harry Ireland, who lived at Church Farm Bungalows near the Black Horse, celebrated their Golden Wedding anniversary on 21 October 1957.

Of the children, she said 'Ken was the oldest one – he was a right dozy devil but he got on well.   He learnt a lot of languages and that, and he used to ride around on a bike with a book up in front of him because in those days there was nothing much on the road.   Fred was the tiny one.   There was this saying, "Mmm, little Baker boy", because he was so tiny.'   Rene remembers being told about the Baker children coming into the baker's shop in Walberton when her parents kept it.   'They used to pester my Mum. They used to wait for Dad to go out and they'd say, "Mrs 'Peppers' (young Fred couldn't say 'Pethers'), have you got any jam tarts or doughnuts?"   If he came back they'd run like hell.'

Fred's brother Bill still lives in Binsted and he remembered his family as follows (interviewed by Bob Davies):

I was born in 1909.   In 1911 the family moved from Newbury to West Walberton Lane in Walberton, and my father worked as a gamekeeper for Colonel Henty who owned the Avisford Estate.   In 1916 my father was called up into the Army.   He was wounded twice (one of the injuries was quite serious) and whilst he was away, in 1917, the Avisford estate was sold to Mr Fairweather.   The family had to move into Walberton, living in Laurel Cottage near the playing field.   My father returned from the war in 1919 and luckily was able to continue to work as a gamekeeper in the Binsted area, this time for Mr Fairweather.

During the early 1920s Mr Fairweather had financial problems and both my father and the head gardener were put on half wages and were allowed to use whatever means available to make up their money.   In the case of my father, he organised more shoots.   For a short time, between 1921 and 1923, my father also worked for a Mr Fairbanks.   He was an

American who had shooting rights over some of the land around Binsted. He also kept some pigs in a field off Church Lane [Muddy Lane].

When Sir Sidney Wishart took over Church Farm my father worked for him for a while. However, the Duke of Norfolk's gamekeeper, Mr Reeves, killed himself and when they decided to replace him my father was offered the job. In 1929/1930 when my father became Gamekeeper for the Duke, the family moved to a house in Tortington (Binsted Lane East), now known as Pinewoods, and my father remained there for the rest of his working life and in his retirement. In those days it was two cottages. The Bakers lived in one, and the other was occupied by Arthur Trusler, who was a foreman at the chalk quarry near the Black Rabbit in Arundel. My father, Charles, died in 1959, my mother, Blanche, in 1960.

There were nine children: Ken, Bill, Charlie, Sidney, Linda, Ron, Eddie, Mabel and Fred. I can remember groceries being delivered from Forest Store, Littlehampton, in a horse-drawn vehicle in 1916, and being taken with Ken to Chichester Hospital in a horse-drawn ambulance when we had scarlet fever.

Rene married Fred and her eldest son Colin was born in 1953 at the Black Horse. Bill Pethers, interviewing her, recalled: 'I remember you having Colin and I was rushed off to school. Nan was rushing about and I could hear the bellows from upstairs!'

Colin Baker

In 1998 Colin Baker, by then assistant Africa Director to the charity ActionAid, was killed when the restaurant in Nairobi where he was eating was raided by armed robbers. They ordered everyone to lie down; for some reason Colin did not do so, and was shot. The moving book of news cuttings and condolences which Rene still treasures reminds us how much he achieved in his short lifetime. He had joined ActionAid in 1989 and worked in Mozambique; later he moved to Malawi, where 'his involvement in ActionAid's Seeds Programme ensured the survival of more than one million families during one of the East African nation's worst droughts'. In 1994 he led emergency work in Goma among Rwandan refugees forced into Zaire. Two years later, he was appointed director of the organisation's Burundi operation. He had been Assistant Director for Africa for two months when he was killed.

Colin Baker at Ruyigi in Burundi in 1995. The occasion was the meeting of local villages for a dance and cultural festival organised by ActionAid.

A colleague, Richard Graham, remembered staying with Colin in Burundi. 'When he showed me round the ActionAid programme, he did so with such commitment, such zeal…I worried that he was working too hard, that he gave almost too much of himself to his work. But …in the circumstances, it must be hard to switch off, and say 'That's the end of my working day, now it's play time'. I left Burundi feeling humbled and deeply impressed.' Richard wrote a poem which captures the sense of waste in Colin's early death, and pictures him relaxing in the way he often did not have time to do:

In a drawer/ In a desk/ In an empty room/ A photo album/ Half-full of pictures:/ A barbecue on a cloudy day/ A blurred runner crossing the finishing line/ The pet dog on the lawn

It's so easy to die/When you least expect it/ With a half-finished game of pool/ Half-finished beer in your hand/ Half-finished sentence hanging in the air

Everything, everything,/ Halved

Half a photo album of blank white leaves/ That will forever remain untouched.

Another colleague, Patricia Balcazar, wrote: 'He was an exceptional person, an inspiring and dedicated colleague who will be sorely missed by ActionAid and all those he worked tirelessly to help in the field.'   Through ActionAid, the Prince of Wales sent a personal message of sympathy and appreciation to Colin's family and to all who worked with him in Kenya.   And the 'entire ActionAid family' sent a message including the words:

It hit us like a thunderbolt!/ We wished it was false,/ But alas, it is true. / Could a man be ripped off/ His life just like that?/ Oh, what can we say?...

Colin Baker, rest in peace,/ Demirifa due,/ Due-due-due,/ Demirifa due.

Like his grandparents, Colin Baker was 'generous to extremes'.

Rene tells a nice story about something Lorna Wishart said to her after Colin's ashes had been scattered in Bill Baker's woods behind the bungalow known as Lake Copse. 'Lorna Wishart said to me one day, "Well, Colin and Wish had a fight at one time, and now they are close together," because Colin's ashes are in Bill's woods and Mr Wishart's are further over.   "They are bound to have settled," she said.'

Living at Morley's Croft *Shelagh Archer*

I moved to Morley's Croft (thought to be a 16th-century cottage) in 1958, at the age of 8 years, with my parents and spent 36 very happy years there.   My father retired from the RAF and started up a small-holding with pigs and chickens on the land beside the cottage.   I remember my father having to take me through Binsted Park to catch the bus to school.   The bus stop was outside the White Swan public house (now called The Mill House), lit by gas in those days.   The road up through the Park was very rough and full of potholes even then.   I was always afraid the car would topple into the 'bottomless pond' as it always seemed to lurch to the left as we were passing it!   There were two old cottages where 'Pinewoods' is now standing, both lit by gas, where Fred Baker (Rene Baker's late husband) lived at the time with his family.

I remember often playing along the bank by the stream at the bottom of the hill past Morley's Croft, which is a tributary of the River Arun.   Apparently Morley's Croft was said to have been a cottage used by smugglers and there is a 'look-out' window in the main bedroom and roof space (now visibly blocked in) to the River Arun to watch for smugglers coming in with their contraband.   Some of the main beams in the cottage were said to have come from ancient shipwrecks and there are still some unusual fittings and handles attached that may have been associated with the sea.

Morley's Croft, where Styles, the Read family's groom, lived.

When we first moved to Morley's Croft, the house opposite to us called Meadow Lodge (which was occupied by Mr. Crisp, his two children, and Miss Pennell, his housekeeper) was so overgrown with bushes and brambles you could barely see it, but over the years it has completely changed – for the better thankfully!

I remember (when I was old enough of course) my first visit to the Black Horse was quite an experience. It was something like going into Aladdin's cave! It was crammed with old cinema seats, very murky paintwork and subdued lighting. Mr. Pethers, the landlord, was elderly then; his hand shook so much, you only got half the drink you had ordered. The rest was all over the bar counter, but he certainly always made you very welcome.

My mother was very friendly with Mrs. Drury (wife of the late Rector of Binsted) and her sister Miss Whitworth, and we quite often went to the Rectory for tea on a Sunday afternoon. I particularly remember the delicate, crustless cucumber sandwiches served by Jane Ellcombe, the maid, whose brother Bill lived in Kent's Cottage in Binsted Park.

I also remember having great fun playing with Alison Sinclair (who lived in Grove Cottages) in the hay barn next to 'Bee Bee Kennels' when it belonged to Mr. Nielsen from Mill Ball. There was a milking shed attached. It has now all been converted to a beautiful home. What a transformation.

Vicki Bryceson and I used to play down by the Rife past Marsh Farm and then go back to Glebe House for china tea and ginger cake. When overseen by her stern father, we frequently developed an attack of the giggles, which we still can do today without any trouble, especially at the Strawberry Fair.

Whilst living in Binsted over the years, we experienced a variety of weather. I remember the big freeze in 1962. The snow fell heavily on Boxing Day and lay on the ground until the end of March. Our then neighbour from Meadow Lodge, Brigadier Leahy, called over to see how we were managing and said to my father, 'Power, we must pool our resources'. We had chickens, eggs and pigs, and to our knowledge his only commodity was large quantities of horse manure from his daughter Amanda's horse called Monty! Cars were left on the lane completely covered with snow, as the wind had blown all the snow off the fields making huge snowdrifts. It was very difficult feeding and watering the animals. My father had to break the ice in the stream next to the pigsties for water and walk across fields to collect food. I couldn't go to school for over a week which pleased me immensely.

Then there was the hurricane in 1987 when I thought the cottage was going to take off. The wind blew one side and took all the tiles off the roof, then as the eye of the storm passed over went round and did the same the other side. Even our bed shook as we lay in it – I don't know how the windows didn't blow out. The sky was bright blue in the middle of the night caused by failing power cables. The electricity and telephone were off for over a week. So many lovely trees came down including many huge oaks and a very tall redwood at the Old Rectory.

Then in 1992 we had torrential rain which went on for 40 or so days causing the stream at the bottom of the hill to flood and come half way up the field. The water was like a river running down Binsted Lane. I had never seen anything like it before. It was gushing past the house on one side – luckily the cottage is on top of a slight hill so it went straight past down the road. I was mopping up water in the kitchen all night, as the water level was so high it was coming up from under the ground.

Morley's Croft was a very comfortable cottage to live in. As the walls were built so thick it was lovely and cool in the summer (particularly the summer of 1976) and cosy in the winter as the thick walls retained the heat. One did, however, have a lot of company in the winter as many mice regularly moved in!

The biggest changes that I have seen in the village over the years were when Rosemary and David Tristram moved into The Rectory. They oversaw the maintenance and improvement to Binsted Church and organised the strawberry fairs, harvest supper and barn dances, which have really made the village into a friendly and close community.

Binsted 1979 to 1995: a personal memory   *Jane Hollowood*

As we followed the removal van up the lane, the children bounced around in the back of the car in a state of wild impatience, but the van, more used to London traffic, proceeded with maddening caution, edging around the hairpin bends at Mount Pleasant and past Grove Cottages, stopping for tractors and the Marsh Farm milking herd, at last making it to 'our' end of the village, up a weedy drive, past a broken gate and the giant overgrown bay tree (long gone now) on the front lawn to draw to a halt outside our new home, Meadow Lodge.

The year is 1979. There are six of us, my husband Jeremy Barlow and our four children. We are moving to the country. I am 38, the children are 11, 8, 7 and 5 and this is the start of a thrilling adventure.

Binsted in 1979 was not particularly pretty. We thought it was magical of course, but love is blind, and friends coming to inspect the move were less rapturous. With hindsight they were probably right.

For a start there were the dead elms. Dutch Elm disease had ravaged Binsted in the mid seventies and by the end of the decade hundreds of beautiful trees, big trees that had given the village its character, were lost. Everywhere you looked, there were rows of stark silhouettes dominating the landscape, waiting to be felled.

Almost as soon as we moved (this sort of thing never happened again, I hasten to add) we managed to have a row over these dead elms. Setting out with a chain saw to cut down the trees along our boundary, we coincided with a couple of men sent by the owner of the adjacent field, also armed with chain saws. Both factions were after firewood and an unseemly dispute took place in which my husband was accused of being a 'lying whelk'. There was no good answer to this, so a compromise was quickly reached and a chainsaw massacre avoided.

A footnote on elms from John North; he estimates that, working for the farm, with a tractor he personally felled some 600 dead elm trees around Binsted in the years that followed the Dutch Elm Disease epidemic.

Snow-covered elms, now gone, in Binsted valley near the Black Horse pub.

As well as dead trees, there were deserted buildings – Binsted at that time seemed to have an unusual number of them – empty barns (barn conversions were a thing of the future), crumbling turkey sheds (Fairmeads Farm), semi-derelict houses ('The Screens', empty and unkempt, the little bungalow next to Bee Bee Kennels, built and never lived in because of a planning hiccup, Kent's Cottage, crumbling away to nothing) and these added to the general air of neglect. In fact down our end of the lane even the lived-in houses didn't look too good. Bee Bee Kennels was distinctly down at heel, Meadow Lodge had ugly 'replacement' picture windows at the front and an overgrown garden divided up by numerous bits of leaning larch lap fencing, and old Henry Pethers' house at the far end of the lane looked as if no-one lived there at all, even though his big black dog could be heard barking from inside. Beyond Mr Pethers' house the track led to the Ruin and the air of neglect gave way to a definite spookiness.

The Ruin had been a grand country house with gardens and stables and a ha-ha. Now it was a tumble of walls and chimney stacks covered in ivy and Virginia creeper and bramble. In what must once have been gardens there were huge trees, deep, open wells and, each spring, the most miraculous carpet of snowdrops. The whole place was bounded by a crumbling brick wall (the bricks were handmade and rather beautiful) and from time to time whole sections of this would disappear, after which the Ruin's owner and guardian, Lorna Wishart, would pin up angry handwritten notes, addressed to the thieves. 'Keep your ******* hands off my bricks!'

The Ruin gave my children nightmares (those wells, that hollow tree just about to fall) at night but by day it became a place of daring and trespass, a glorious and strictly forbidden playground.

Beside the Ruin lay another spooky Binsted wonder, the Madonna Pond. In those days it was entirely overhung with trees and always dark even on the brightest day. The water was a thick and sinister black, criss-crossed with dead branches you could balance along. No-one knew how deep the water was, but the presumption was that if you fell in, you'd disappear for ever. Actually it was only a few feet.

Presiding over the pond that spring was Lorna Wishart's first and finest Madonna - life size and painted (pretty pink face, pretty blue robes). Later someone was to come along and, rather horribly, chop off her head and she had to be replaced. The new one was much smaller and encased in a thick, vandal-proof wrapping of wire.

The pond naturally had ghosts. It was haunted (a coach and four had sunk into it without trace, etc.); black magic was known to have taken place on its banks ('definite evidence' found, bloodied prams with sacrificial pheasants, actually left by local poachers). On Halloween Night the big dare in our family was to walk past the pond in the dark. No-one ever succeeded.

Lorna Wishart, wife of Ernest, owner of Marsh and Church Farms, was I'm afraid to say another spooky element from the children's point of view. As she rattled past Meadow Lodge several times each day in her red Land Rover, up to her garden in the woods, she seemed, with her long black hair, red lipstick, black mascara and haughty green eyes, the very epitome of a witch, a thought which would probably have amused her greatly. In fact, of course, she was always very kind to our children, picking them up off the road when they fell off their bikes, lending tiny lace hankies to dry their eyes and so on, and had been an enormous beauty in her day.

So, we found ourselves living tucked away at the far end of this slightly derelict, excitingly spooky village. We did not have a good start. Almost at once, the heavens opened and we had a fortnight of torrential rain which caused our cellar to flood, saturating the contents of our packing cases, stored there while we had a new staircase put in. But in spite of this BINSTED seemed a very good place to be.

The children started at their new schools, the younger ones (Marian, Dan and Jos) to the village school in Walberton under its headteacher Mr Golder, the eldest (Tom) to Bishop Luffa, and I found a room in the village in which to work. Each morning we would all set off, me pushing my bike, the younger three trotting alongside, to wait for the school bus outside Grove Lodge. The two Davey boys, Philip and Andrew, would be waiting too, and further down the lane there would be Nicky Baker and, later, Tracey Pethers, waiting outside Oakleys, and Suzanne, Jo and Steve Kemp and Tracey Lamb outside the pub. Binsted provided quite a busload of children in those days and they were kept in order by a Mrs Aslett who drove the bus and ruled it with a firm hand. Meanwhile our oldest son would cycle to Beam Ends, leave his bike behind Mrs Watts's shed and catch a different school bus to Chichester – much more of a journey in those days with no Fontwell bypass and only one short stretch of dual carriageway between Walberton and Chi.

As soon as the children had left for school, I cycled on to my new work room just down the road. Perhaps I should explain at this point that I was (and still am) a television script writer and that my then husband was a musician who needed to practice his flute and piano each morning. The layout of Meadow Lodge is compact and two people, especially if one is playing major and minor scales on the piccolo and the other is bashing away on the typewriter (pre-computer days these), cannot get out of sound-range of each other. Something had to give. One day I had a message from Niels Nielsen at Mill Ball. We'd never met but he'd heard I needed a room. Would his spare bedroom do?

I moved in a few days later and perched my typewriter on an old Singer sewing machine table that stood in the window, thinking that the arrangement would never last, that this kindly old man would very soon get sick of a stranger in his house. I ended up staying until his death in 1990 and always smile to think of the dozens of episodes of Eastenders, the ultimate urban soap, that were written in that room, overlooking the rural bliss of Niels's garden.

Knowing Niels was one of the nicest things about my time in Binsted. Originally from Denmark but stranded in Binsted 'by Hitler' (as he put it with his usual innocent smile), he was an exceptionally sweet-natured and hospitable man. His open house 'elevenses' were famous. Each day at eleven on the dot, people appeared like magic. Niels would set the tray and with his cry of 'It's at its best!' summon them in to sit at his big round table for coffee, homemade cakes (often supplied by Peggy North) and biscuits. Talk would be wide ranging. Niels liked, in his gentle way, to start a good discussion and I remember animated discussions about the poll tax and Margaret Thatcher and the Arundel Bypass. Niels and I would often disagree violently but there was always a twinkle in his eye.

As spring advanced that first year, the true beauty of Binsted began to show itself. It was a magical place after all. In the late seventies it was still very much an agricultural community, dominated by the farming year and the rhythm of the seasons. The major landowner and farmer was, as now, the Wishart family, who owned much of the land and eleven farm cottages up and down the lane, many of which still had farm workers living in them. The farm itself still employed a full time manager, who lived at Walberton Farm, and ten or so full time workers. Today I believe there are no full time workers at all.

The only other farm of any size was Mill Ball, owned by Niels. In his heyday he'd been a major player in the village, keeping a pedigree jersey herd and farming all the fields to the left of the lane from the Rectory upwards, as far north as Spinning-Wheel Copse, as far east as the water meadows between Meadow Lodge and Goose Green. He owned Flint Barn, where he kept his hay and calves, and Slated Barn, now converted into a house, where he did the milking and cream making. But by '79, Niels was in his late sixties and in the process of winding down. The cows had gone and he was gradually selling off his fields and concentrating on growing fruit at his beloved Mill Ball. His orchards, a mass of blossom in the spring, grew mostly apples and raspberries (the picking season was frantic, everybody helped) but also pears, damsons, plums, figs and peaches.

Most of the other small farm enterprises were by this time just a memory, having died out in the fifties and sixties: Paddy Power with his pig farm at Morley's Croft, the Hoods, who lived in a railway carriage opposite Oakley Cottages and had a milking herd, the turkey farm at Fairmeads. But new enterprises were starting up. Binsted Herbs was beginning to employ people in a small way on its one field site alongside the Rectory, and elsewhere in Binsted we were witnessing an early sortie into the world of organic farming, as the Wishart farm manager, Tom Haslett, took over land to grow organic crops. Fields were planted with organic garlic and raspberries; a worm farm with worms especially collected from France was set up in heaps of dung across the road from Oakleys. Unfortunately these enterprises were overtaken by weeds and the worms disappeared, perhaps back to France.

As a place to grow up in, Binsted was unsurpassed. Twenty years ago children were allowed to roam around the countryside in a way that doesn't happen any more. In fact, parents positively ordered their children 'out to play' and then didn't expect to see them till the next meal! And in Binsted, there were so many places to go. Binsted Woods, where you could quite easily imagine yourself lost and where, somewhere, hidden away, you knew Lorna Wishart had her Secret Garden, if only you could find it, the Ruin, the pond, the rife and its tributaries for paddling and raft building, the very interesting contents of Mr Pearce's and Mr Baker's sheds to examine (apologies to both gentlemen. I didn't know at the time) including , excitingly, the late Colin Baker's life size model of a nuclear missile which he used to take on Greenham Common marches. And then of course there were the more dangerous and the strictly out of bounds pleasures of Church and Marsh Farms where I'm afraid to say my children secretly played a truly terrifying game called 'crossing the slurry pit', a game I never knew about till years later and which I can now hardly bear to think about.

Finally and perhaps best of all, there was Niels's wood, to which he allowed my children unlimited access, a truly idyllic wood with streams and a pond, islands and little bridges and in spring, a mass of flowers, primroses, bluebells, early purple orchids along the stream (every year we used to count them and every year they'd increased, up to, I think, about sixty plants), and daffodils. Many happy hours were spent making camps on the islands.

And there was the wildlife to enjoy, particularly the birds, a huge variety, a bird watcher's delight. I remember Binsted for cuckoos in spring, dozens of them calling from all around, and above all for nightingales. In those days there were nightingales everywhere, in Hedgers Hill and behind Sandhole Pond, in Spinning-Wheel Copse, in the scrub at Fairmeads Farm, below Henry Pethers' house. We used to like awake at Meadow Lodge and hear three or four singing at once and I remember old Mr Pethers telling me that he had to shut his bedroom window to get any sleep, they sang so close and loud. Sadly, and I do not know why, by the time we left Binsted in '95, the nightingales had gone and the cuckoo had become a rarity.

Vast snowdrift in Binsted Lane in the early 1980s.

And then there were the weather excitements. Rare spectacular falls of snow, including one in the early eighties when the lane had drifts 5 feet high and the snow lasted for weeks and weeks; the flooding then freezing of the water meadows when we would dig out our ancient skates and spend all afternoon on the ice until the sun set red; the incredible Great Storm of the night of 17 October 1987, during which my daughter came into our bedroom in the early hours with the classic words 'I think it's a bit windy' and together she and I stood at a window and watched as whole oak trees crashed to the ground along the edge of Meadow Lodge's water meadow and the big old crack willow tree in the garden bent trunk and all in the strongest gusts. In the morning there was no electricity or telephone (and wouldn't be for many days) and I remember us and our neighbours from Bee Bee Kennels and Morley's Croft huddling around a battery tranny to hear what was going on in the outside world. Binsted Woods were almost unrecognisable with mature beeches and oaks uprooted everywhere and the track past the pond blocked by so many fallen trees that we thought it could never be opened again.

So the years passed. The Country Fair of 1983, ably organised by Peggy North, came and went. Annual village events – Strawberry Fairs, Carol Services with the Tristrams' mince pie and mulled wine party afterwards, Harvest Suppers in Flint Barn, Barn Dances (very jolly with live bands and, ambitiously in its first year, two Meadow Lodge lambs roasted on a spit) – became established.

Then the children grew to be teenagers and suddenly the attractions of Binsted, for them at least, waned. Life became a worrying time for parents, a time of mopeds and motorbikes and old bangers and three a.m. phone calls to report 'being stuck' at some remote spot and needing picking up.

And then they left home altogether.

All except the youngest who went to university and speedily came back again, choosing instead to live alone in a shed at the bottom of a field below Fairmeads, with his guitar and a supply of porridge oats. Happily, after eighteen months of this, he went back to his studies but I like to think that Binsted prepared him excellently for his present life in the Brazilian Rainforest.

And once they'd all gone, it seemed time to leave the big old house at the end of the lane and do something new. Binsted had changed a lot. Many of the old timers had died – Niels, Ernest and Lorna Wishart, Henry Pethers. Others had moved away. The deserted barns had become houses, new trees were growing in place of the dead elms, the farm workers had left, the small village pub had turned into an eating place, there was a golf course! But in essence it is still the same. The woods, the rife, the fields…the things that really matter, will go on. As the countryside between the Downs and the sea becomes more and more built up, it's still a pretty amazing oasis.

It always used to be said that if you lived too long in Binsted, particularly at its far end, you either took to drink or went mad. I don't think I took to drink but maybe I did stay too long – my next move, to a remote farm on the edge of Exmoor to farm at a time when farmers are going bust, certainly smacks of madness.

Havest Supper in the Flint Barn.

Chapter 7
'Friends of Binsted Church' and Binsted Nursery

Mike Tristram with Rosemary Tristram

In the 1970s the spire and roof of Binsted's twelfth-century church needed repairing. The last Rector's daughter, Janet Whiting, sold the Old Rectory, opposite the church, in 1973. The coach-house and stables made a small home for Hubert and Emily Roberts, and the rest of the Rectory a larger one for their daughter Rosemary, her husband David Tristram, and their three children, Ruth, myself and Frances. David bought nearby Homestead Nursery on Yapton Lane from the Walbrughs and renamed it Walberton Nursery, starting with growing then-fashionable conifers and later adding more exciting plants bred or introduced by himself.

First Hubert Roberts, and later David Tristram, became churchwardens. Hubert and Emily started 'after-church breakfasts' which increased numbers attending. But how, in our small village, to raise enough money for the repairs? Outsiders' money had to be lured in.

Friends of Binsted Church

The village got together to put on a Herb Festival in the churchyard, on 15th June 1977. Rosemary, Janet Whiting and friends produced all sorts of herbs in pots on Walberton Nursery, grown from seeds and from cuttings scrounged from anyone with a garden and herb plants to spare, while others made various herb products such as jellies, jams, biscuits, teas, cakes and herb bread, and these were sold together with a herb recipe booklet. The booklet had over 30 recipes headed as Soups and Vegetables, Main Dishes, Cakes Puddings etc, Butters Cheeses and Sauces, and Beverages, with Harvesting, Drying and General Hints. Here's a sample one – appropriately,

Rosemary Biscuits

4 oz butter	2 oz sugar
6 oz flour	2 tbsp chopped rosemary

Cream butter and sugar. Add flour and rosemary. Knead well into a dough.
Roll out and cut into shapes. Bake at 4500F oven for 10-12 mins (2300C, Gas mark 8).

In 1980 the church spire was repaired and re-shingled. The whole community, irrespective of religious denominations or beliefs, had got together to raise the money needed, but this new income sparked off impossible demands for increased general annual parish 'quota' payments to the Church Commissioners. To allow the village to keep control of its fund-raising for chosen causes, whether sacred or secular, a new association, the 'Friends of Binsted Church', was formed in 1981. The Herb Festival

The weathercock of Binsted church, taken down from the steeple during work in 1996.

was the first of many fund-raising events on behalf of Binsted church and other good causes, which were later held in the Flint Barn and field, 'Herb Festival' giving way to 'Country Fair' and then to 'Strawberry Fair'. Binsted Nursery still makes available the barn and a polytunnel each summer for the Strawberry Fair, and Binsted and Walberton Nurseries donate plants for sale there which contribute to the Friends' income. This goes to the upkeep of the church, with any extra being given to charities.

A table of events held by the Friends of Binsted Church, showing how much money was spent on the church, and what it was spent on, makes clear how much attention this old building has needed (and continues to need), and the fun and hard work that have gone into looking after it.

1981 Inaugural meeting, 24/3. Antiques Road Show, 25/7. Tea party held by Peggy North, 25/7. Concert given by Jeremy Barlow, 11/9. *Repairs to roof, gutters, downpipes, perimeter wall, gate, subsidence by N wall.*

1982 Auction at the Black Horse (Oct). *Rentokil treatment of all woodwork (25-year guarantee), repairs to gutters, tiles, flint and stonework, drainage channels, walls, buttress, plasterwork and leaded windows. Decoration by volunteers.* £635.

1983 Concert given by Jeremy Barlow, 15/7. Country Fair, 10/9. Auction at Black Horse. *Twelfth-century wall painting preserved by Fiona Allardyce.* £500.

1984 Nursery Open Day 18/8. Harvest Supper 15/9. *Floor taken up N side, also in vestry, supporting timber replaced with pressure-treated timber, dampcourse installed. N side gutter renewed. New bellrope. Dangerous tree felled.* £1,070.

1985 Talk on Nigeria by Ray Geale 13/2. Concert by Jeremy Barlow 25/10. Harvest Supper 14/9. *Polycarbonate screens fitted to all windows other than those with grilles.* £453.

1986 Nursery Open Day 19/7. *Repairs to flintwork, especially W wall, repointing, treating with water repellent. Repairs to porch woodwork, lead flashing round spire. Decorating by volunteers.* £1,075.

1987 Nursery Open Day arranged for Oct 16, but prevented by hurricane. *Continuation of above work.*

1988 Strawberry Fair 3/7. Nursery Open Day 17/9. *Repairs to plaster. Decoration by volunteers.* £89.

1989 Strawberry Fair 2/7, and storm damage insurance money. *Entire church re-roofed. Repairs to gutters, downpipes, perimeter wall.* £8,865.

1990 Strawberry Fair 8/7. Concert by Jeremy Barlow 1/9.

1991 Strawberry Fair 30/6. *New stone surround for W window, its leaded glass remade. More repointing of W wall and water-repellent treatment. Repairs to buttresses, quoins, windows and perimeter wall.* £6,234.

1992 Harvest Supper 19/9. *Continuation of above work.*

1993 Strawberry Fair 4/7.   Harvest Supper 18/9.   *Electrical wiring survey carried out.*
£100.
1994 Strawberry Fair 3/7.   *Estimates for new work accepted but builders failed to start.*
1995 Strawberry Fair 9/7.   *Church completely rewired, and new notice-board by road.*
Building work plans rejected by Diocese.   £2,411.
1996 Strawberry Fair 14/7.   *Injection of damp course, replastering lower parts of walls and*
redecorating, repairs to steeple, vestry, buttresses, gutters, stonework, windows, perimeter wall,
credence, box tombs.   New kneelers.   Pews re-varnished.   C. £14,000.
1997 Strawberry Fair 6/7.   *New pew, panelling and other repairs, architects' fees.*   £1,670.
1998 Strawberry Fair 19/7.   *Repairs to windows, roof, painting etc.*   £1,701.
1999 Strawberry Fair 18/7.   *Repairs to guttering, organ repaired.*   £1,070.
2000 Strawberry Fair 2/7.   *Repairs to porch etc.*   £814.
2001 Strawberry Fair 8/7.   *Replaced alms box and sundry repairs.*   £197.

The church is still used for services, currently once a month, with major festival services at Harvest, Christmas and Easter, when it is beautifully decorated.   On Rogation Sunday a procession crosses the valley from Walberton to Binsted and can be heard singing as it approaches.   The church is used by the community as a whole for meetings, such as meetings about the Arundel Bypass and the South Downs National Park, and the 'Millennium meeting' which inaugurated this book.

Herbs and horses

Binsted Nursery had its origins in the Herb Festival, but also in the oil crisis of the 1970s and friends made through riding.   Rosemary writes:

When we first arrived in Binsted, we bought a horse for the children, partly to compensate for bringing them away from Southern Ireland, where we had all been very happy.   We had two or three wonderful years riding through the woods, and down to the sea and up to the Signpost on the Downs.   When the oil crisis hit us I spent much of my time weeding at Walberton Nursery, and out of kindness the friends I had made over saddles and hay bales (Joan, Janet, Judy and Gillian) joined in, though the Nursery was unable to pay them at the time.   However, when the crisis passed and times became easier, David was able to pay us all, and then on wet days he had to give us something else to do, which is how we came to know something about growing when the Herb Festival came along.

One of the great pleasures of building up numbers and varieties of plants for that first event was the people we met, all extremely generous with seeds, cuttings and advice.   I have very happy memories of gathering huge quantities of red and variegated sage cuttings from Mrs Barren's lovely old walled garden in Madehurst.   The advice did not prevent our making some mistakes which, given our ignorance at the time, was hardly surprising.   I remember discussing whether a particular batch of plants really were the best, French form of tarragon, only to be told discreetly on the day by someone more knowledgeable that it wasn't tarragon at all – the labels had to be swiftly removed!

It seems a considerable leap from this very amateur beginning to going into wholesale production of herbs for the Garden Centre market, but this arose because we had grown the plants for the Festival on Walberton Nursery, where they were spotted by the Farplants sales representatives. Although these first plants were grown in spent compost and used pots, they liked what they saw and as they were certain that there was a future for herbs in the wholesale market, they suggested that we might grow herbs for them. At that time, Walberton Nursery was rapidly filling the land it then owned and David was looking for a crop to grow on one of our fields at Binsted - and so the Binsted herb partnership came into being, with Janet Whiting and myself growing the plants and David giving technical and practical advice and support.

I still remember the excitement of moving plants over into our own (second-hand) glass-houses, and then the various milestones - the first whole lorry load of plants going out, the first trays of alpines laid out in flower and bud for collection by Farplants (much prettier than the herbs to my mind, but sadly to prove much less profitable), the first order worth £1000, the venture into marketing direct to Covent Garden, the first hardy male employees(!) and of course our involvement with the British Herb Trade stand at Chelsea and seeing our plants on TV one year, as part of their Silver Medal winning display.

Nursery slopes

In 1978, commercial production of herbs began in borrowed facilities at Walberton Nursery, and in 1979 the first pots of herbs stood in Binsted fields. The breeze-block shelter for animals was turned into a rest-room with a camping toilet in a lean-to out the back. Plants were grown in some wooden 'Dutch light' glasshouses and under home-made polythene-clad 'cloches' as well as outdoors, on sand-beds. Soon after, some polytunnels and a shade-house were added. There followed ten years of hard graft as Rosemary and Janet worked with friends and gradually more employees to turn an idea into a business. The nursery remained a women's enterprise for a number of years. And it was very much a family business: in the early days, labels were mostly written and bundled by hand by my grandmother Emily Roberts, sitting in Stable Cottage's sun-room looking over to the nursery.

All kinds of herbs, medicinal and culinary, were tried out, gradually rising to over 100 varieties. New varieties were in demand and selected forms were introduced including a new variety of spearmint Rosemary brought back from Tashkent (now widely sold as 'Tashkent Mint'). Seeds were collected here from herbs growing in beds (many were not commercially obtainable in those days), and cleaned through sieves in the Old Rectory kitchen – a nice warm job on cold winter days, much enjoyed by those who didn't mind getting dust in their noses.

To begin with, the garden centres wanted more herbs than growers could supply, so very little of what was produced got wasted, and the nursery prospered. Next, garden centres wanted alpines along with the herbs. Many alpines are seductively lovely bright gems, but not always easy to grow. Managing the complex production planning for so many varieties of herbs and alpines, often with numerous batches per variety each year, became a nightmare - and usually had to be done at night after an exhausting day's physical work.

The hurricane and its aftermath

Then came the October 1987 hurricane. It left the nursery and in fact the whole village devastated by huge fallen trees, even though the gigantic elms formerly surrounding the Old Rectory's fields had already come down with Dutch Elm Disease in the 1970s.

Rosemary remembers: *One day still stands out more clearly than any other - October 16th 1987, with the wind roaring like a non-stop express train and desolation all about us, tunnels reduced overnight to twisted metal and scraps of plastic, 2000 polystyrene trays vanished with only a tell-tale few caught up along the edge of the woods to show where all the rest had gone, and yesterday's boundary row of pine trees flattened and embedded in rows of crushed and jumbled pots of plants. All through the morning, staff appeared after walking (all the roads being blocked by fallen trees) from as far away as Littlehampton, just to see if there was anything that they could do to help.*

Even today I sometimes see a moss-covered bit of tray in the depths of Binsted Woods, blown there in 1987 or in the action replay we experienced in 1990. The cost of the hurricane and of the increasing complexity of the business were hard to bear financially but the stress hit morale hard too. The nursery was producing plants to be proud of, but not profits. After several difficult years, Janet Whiting retired. Meanwhile I had left my job editing children's books in London and re-trained in commercial horticulture, finishing in summer 1989. In that year my grandparents took the decision to move out of Stable Cottage while they were still fit and well into an independent flat in a nursing home in Aldwick. Emma and I moved into Stable Cottage and I joined Binsted Herbs (as it was then still called). Rosemary initiated me into the business and then generously took a back seat, giving me a free hand while she continued to do her least favourite job, the paperwork, until she 'retired' to work for SSAFA (Forces Help).

Change and growth

In 1989 the nursery was selling about a quarter of a million plants a year each of herbs and alpines. I worked at improving our marketing, for instance with picture labels. We changed the variety mix and growing regime, and learnt to delegate. We were selling over three-quarters of a million plants by 1993, but not profitably enough. So we made a radical decision – we stopped growing alpines, though they made up half our turnover at the time.

In alpines' place we put spring bulbs, perennials, and autumn patio plants. Developing these new ranges wasn't easy at first. For spring bulbs, we tried 95 varieties in small pots in year one, then the best 65 the next year, then the best 35 including some larger one-litre pots the next year; now we do large numbers of just 12 varieties of spring bulbs (daffodils, tulips, windflowers, grape hyacinths), all in bigger pots. I bought in hundreds of unusual perennials every year, and tried all sorts of different ways to grow them, to find out what we could offer to garden centres that would sell really well and that they wouldn't readily get from other nurseries. In 1995-97, half the plants we sold each year were new or recently added crops. Over the 5 years to 1998 we doubled our turnover, while reducing the number of varieties we grew from around 500 to less than half that.

To cope with this rate of change and growth, the nursery staff developed more specialised roles. Also I had to go part-time due to illness from 1996 and, while I managed to keep up with marketing and the strategic development of the business, the nursery manager (Paul Bennett) and everybody else had to do a lot more. Physical work was made easier with more trailers, trolleys and conveyors, and more tunnels went up to provide protected working spaces for staff as well as growing areas for plants. We got some better growing facilities at last - a new state-of-the-art propagation house we built at Binsted, and a two-acre former carnation nursery that came available to rent in Littlehampton. Then we built a half-acre polytunnel at Binsted with roof and sides automatically opening and closing by computer control according to the weather, a facility undreamt of when we began.

Interesting plants

We still do around 100 varieties of herbs. Our past history of growing alpines can still be seen in some of our lines: Mossy Saxifrage, Snakeshead Fritillary, Dwarf Pinks, Campanulas, Aubrietas, Double Primroses, blue Corydalis, blue perennial Phlox, Garden Celandines including 'Brazen Hussy' (very similar to one found in Lake Copse which we have distributed to specialist nurseries as *Ranunculus ficaria* 'Binsted Woods'). The excitement of breeding new garden plants was caught from my father David, who has introduced great plants at Walberton Nursery such as Spiraea Magic Carpet and Scabious Pink Mist, and goes back to grandfather Guy Tristram who bred Rose Toby Tristram. New plants bred or selected at Binsted include Aquilegia 'Purple Emperor', a columbine with golden foliage and purple-blue flowers, which I bred as a seed strain at Binsted and named for the butterfly which may still inhabit the edges of the woods behind the nursery.

Suddenly the plants we had been developing really took off. Farplants was selling them to garden centres across the whole of Great Britain. We doubled our output again from 1998 to 2000/1. In 2000, we sold our first million pounds' worth of plants in a year (retail value about three million pounds). We are currently producing about 2 million pots a year, of which over 700,000 are still herbs. We have invested in land next to Walberton Nursery at Lake Lane, for Binsted Nursery's expanded production. We have just built a one-acre polytunnel there, the first in the country of its type. While farms employ ever fewer people, there are now about 50 people working at Binsted Nursery in the main growing season. Binsted Nursery and the Friends of Binsted Church may now seem like odd bedfellows, but they are both, in different ways, helping to keep the countryside alive.

Fragaria 'Golden Alexandria', a golden-leaved strain of alpine strawberry bred in Binsted. Its seeds are sold around the world.

Chapter 8   The bypass battle, 1987-93

Emma Tristram

I came to live in Stable Cottage, Binsted, in 1989 with Mike and two children aged seven and three.   I remember looking out of the window at Binsted Woods, an immensely long, dark shape lying beyond the field at the end of our garden, like an immobilized wave in a huge sea.   Rosemary, my mother-in-law, said 'the new road's going to go over there.'

At the time this was true.   The government was planning to put a new trunk road through Binsted, as the Western end of a new Arundel Bypass.   After 'public consultation' (questionnaires through letterboxes showing three possible routes) in 1987, they had chosen as their 'Preferred Route' a monstrosity called the 'Orange Route',

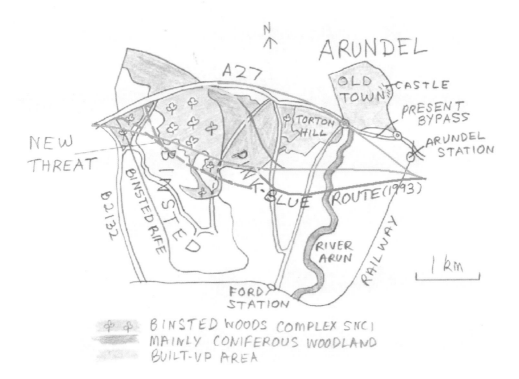

This map shows the routes for the Arundel Bypass offered by the Department of Transport in 1987 (Orange, Purple and Red) and the Pink/Blue route which was made the Preferred Route in 1993. The 'new threat' is the 'Green' routes (first suggested in 1993 and rejected, but revived in 2002).

which might have been designed to cause maximum environmental damage and destroy Binsted as a place. The planners' attitude to Binsted was that it would make a nice view for drivers as they passed through (this suggestion appeared in one of the Department of Transport's expert reports).

The Orange route started with a two-level junction at Avisford, at the north end of Yapton Lane, with access roundabouts either side, and a new slip road at Little Dane's Wood. It virtually obliterated Hundred House Copse (a wet valley and nature reserve), then smashed through all the most sheltered, southwest-facing edges of the main block of Binsted Woods – the best part for both wildlife and walkers. It continued across the southern part of Tortington Common (next to a strip of broad-leaved woodland, the only part of the Common to be included in the Binsted Woods SNCI), passed near the houses of Torton Hill, and then straddled the water-meadows south of Arundel, close to the town.

I became Secretary of the Arundel Bypass Neighbourhood Committee, the local group that had formed to fight the plan. They had been working hard since 1987, with people in Arundel, to get a less damaging bypass. I was soon drafting letters, drawing maps, writing to the papers, organising meetings, taking minutes, delivering leaflets, talking to officials and conservation pressure groups, liaising with Councils, navigating local politics, absorbing the legal processes behind road plans, weighing the arguments for and against new roads, and reading expert botanical reports (I have a large cardboard box full of them). All the drafting was done on an old Olivetti Lettera 22 manual typewriter at the kitchen table.

The result of six years of hard work was that in the summer of 1993, a route called the Pink/Blue route was made the new Preferred Route for the bypass. The Pink (Western) part used most of the existing dual carriageway, avoiding Binsted and Binsted Woods, then turned south through conifer plantations on Tortington Common, which support a far smaller amount of wildlife than Binsted's broad-leaved woods. The route joined up with the Blue route across Arundel's water-meadows (curving much further south than the Orange route), which was what people in Arundel had been asking for since 1990. The Pink route had been suggested in 1991 by our group together with the Sussex Wildlife Trust – a staunch ally from the first, in the person of Frank Penfold, past Chairman of the Trust's Council.

But the road was not built. First the Conservative government dithered (or accepted the advice of its research group, SACTRA, that new roads cause more congestion); then the new Labour government, elected in 1997, wished to save money and appear 'green' by cutting back severely on new roads. Now the government is rumbling back towards a policy of building more new roads. The civil servants are taking out their old files on bypasses and blowing the dust off them.

There is a vocal pro-bypass lobby in Arundel, partly because congestion on the existing bypass, built in the 1960s, drives traffic up into the old town; commuters fret in the twice-daily jams; drivers from Burpham cannot get out onto the A27; and West Sussex County Council has been promoting a new bypass for years as essential for economic development. It seems likely that, sooner or later, the whole tedious, messy battle will start all over again. Now, therefore, is a good time to look back at the previous round in the fight.

1987-9: the Modified Orange Route

1987: 'Not the Red route!'

The three routes offered by the Department of Transport in its 1987 questionnaire were called Orange, Red and Purple.   Orange, described above, was nearly straight, as though a civil servant somewhere had taken a ruler and drawn a line.   Red was different at the Western end: instead of starting at Avisford, it used the current A27 as far as the Arundel Arboretum (a tree nursery), then turned south to join the Orange route, passing close to the houses of Torton Hill.   Purple was essentially an 'upgrading' of the present bypass, but went south of Arundel Station.

All three routes caused alarm and consternation.   The questionnaires had to be returned by 10 July.   On 16 June a meeting was held in Binsted Church.   A committee was formed called the 'Arundel Red Route Campaign', chaired by Jeremy Barlow of Binsted.   From the point of view of people at this end, the Purple (on-line) route would have been best, but politics suggested that this route would not be acceptable in Arundel.   As well as splitting the main part of the town from Torton Hill, and bringing increased noise to the historic, old part of the town, the Purple route provided no solution to the problem of heavy lorries using Ford Road, a narrow residential road. Arundel people for years had been asking for a 'proper bypass', not an upgrading of the present route.

Red was seen as a compromise.   But it soon appeared that even the Red route stood little chance of being accepted in Arundel. The strength of feeling against Red was impressed on members of the Binsted committee when at one meeting there were angry shouts of 'Not the Red route!'

Modified Orange: a solution for both ends

Arundel groups were pressing for a modification to the Orange route at their end to take it further south.   If they could do that, perhaps our end could suggest a modification that took the western section of the road further north-east.   Advice from the Sussex Wildlife Trust was that with a view to protecting the best woodland, the further north-east our part of the road could go, the better.   This also took it further from the village. Thus was the 'Modified Orange Route' (sometimes called MOR) born, originally a new idea for the whole of the bypass, put together at lightning speed by people at Binsted collaborating with Arundel Town Council.   This collaboration seemed a far better bet than a fight to the death between Orange and Red routes, with Arundel pressing for Orange, people this end for Red.   The bypass began to assume the S-shaped curve which later became even more pronounced in the victorious Pink/Blue route.

The name of the Binsted group was changed from 'Arundel Red Route Campaign' to 'Arundel Bypass Neighbourhood Committee' (ABNC), reflecting the fact that Arundel and Binsted were now working together.   An outline of the Modified Orange Route was submitted to West Sussex County Council (agents for the Department of Transport) by the 10 July 1987 deadline, as a result of which the Department of Transport asked the Council to survey the route and prepare costings.   ABNC produced its own questionnaire form allowing people to vote for the Modified Orange Route.   At incredible cost in effort and shoeleather, this leaflet was distributed by members of the group round every house in Arundel, Binsted, Walberton and Slindon.

On June 23rd the Modified Orange Route was approved by a densely packed open meeting held by Arundel Town Council in the Town Hall. On July 6th a crowded open meeting held by Walberton Parish Council in Walberton School endorsed it unanimously. The Modified Orange Route had achieved a certain momentum. But would it survive the arcane decision-making processes of the Department of Transport?

1989: Orange the 'Preferred Route'

The answer was no. In June 1989, the Department of Transport announced that the Orange route had been chosen as the 'Preferred Route'. Reasons were given for rejecting the Modified Orange Route. At the Binsted end, it was rejected because 'it would be nearer to Havenwood Caravan Park and other property, encroach further into the woodland dividing it in two and taking more of it, require a more complex junction at Avisford and achieve less economic benefit.'

How simple things seemed to the Department of Transport in those days. It had no concept of different types of woodland with greatly differing ecological value; and its favourite criterion of 'economic benefit' was based on a cost benefit analysis, or COBA for short, which calculated the amount of time saved by drivers in money terms. The now accepted fact that new roads encourage more traffic, and thus cause more congestion, was not yet part of the equation. Still worse, from the point of view of countryside-lovers, routes that came out best according to COBA involved land that was cheapest to acquire, such as beautiful undeveloped countryside. No wonder it was sometimes mispronounced COBRA.

Havenwood Park, a development of mobile homes in the northernmost part of Binsted Woods, had not been forgotten by the Binsted group; the Modified Orange Route had been designed to go 250m. south of its southernmost point, which was felt to be more favourable than the present position of the A27, a few feet from the most northerly mobile home. The residents did not agree, an important factor in our eventual change to supporting the Pink route.

Analysis of the 1987 questionnaire showed that the Orange route had most support - as was expected, since it was furthest from the town of Arundel, which had the most respondents. As their first choice, 616 put Orange, 223 Purple and 142 Red. On whether people thought their property would be adversely affected, Purple and Orange were more equal (250 for Purple, 208 for Orange).

The Government's choice of the Orange route was extremely unacceptable at both ends of the road. Another round of frenzied activity began. At the Arundel end, a new group known as ABAC (Arundel Bypass Action Committee), founded in January 1990, began an intense campaign for a more southerly route across the water-meadows, known as the Blue route - choosing an even more southerly curve than their end of the MOR had suggested. At the Binsted end, efforts were at first concentrated on trying to get our end of the MOR 'reconsidered'.

Route to the Pink route

It was at this point that we moved to Binsted (August 1989) and I became involved in the campaign. Looking at my large pile of dry-as-dust files, I have decided to tell the rest of the story as a series of meetings.

In June 1991 there was another round of public consultations. Arundel had achieved its Blue route, but at the western end we were only offered the Brown route, hardly different from the dreaded Orange. The questionnaire had to be returned by 9 August.

July 1991: A meeting with Christopher Chope

He was then Junior Minister for Roads in the Department of Transport. Don Milburn, then chairman of Walberton Parish Council, and I met him at the house of our MP, Sir Michael Marshall, who was unfailingly helpful in enabling us to put our views across to the Department of Transport. We were also helped by Alex Moody, our County Councillor. Mr Chope was youngish, slim and genial. He took in what we said, and made a statement to the Press afterwards stating that he had learnt something from us about 'the value of different types of woodland'. We felt slightly hopeful.

July 1991: A meeting with the Department of Transport

This was less cheerful. Luke Wishart, David Tristram and I met two Department of Transport officials at West Sussex County Council, and lobbied for the Modified Orange Route. One official was blunt. He said long stretches of road through woodland (of any kind) were awful. He said mobile homes had thinner walls than normal houses so it was important that the road should be further from Havenwood than from the ancient houses of Binsted. We were asking for our route to be 'reconsidered'. He said the Department might 'consider considering it'.

August 1991: A meeting with Mrs McCormick of Havenwood Park

In the kitchen of Stable Cottage, Binsted, Luke Wishart and I sat down with Mrs McCormick, of the Havenwood Park Residents' Association, to look at the routes. (Luke was now chairman of ABNC as Jeremy Barlow had left Binsted.) ABNC and the Havenwooders had not officially met before - an omission. We wanted to see how Mrs McCormick would react to a new idea from Frank Penfold of the Sussex Wildlife Trust - the Pink route. This was a proposal for a new alignment further east, starting from near the end of the present dual carriageway, and curving south through pinewood plantations to join the Blue route across the Arundel water-meadows.

Mrs McCormick made firm objections to the Modified Orange Route. A new road 250m south of Havenwood would be noisy and leave the residents marooned between two roads. It would not do. We showed her the Pink route. She took in its virtues at once and supported it. She thought most of Havenwood's 100 or so 'souls' would support it, though some turned out to disagree - mainly people from the north end of the Park who suffer road noise from the A27 at present. It was following this crucial meeting that ABNC changed its policy from supporting the Modified Orange Route to proposing the Pink route. Its leaflet 'September update' of 1991 put the arguments.

December 1991: A meeting with our new County Councillor, Harold Hall

A great deal of support for the Pink route came from ecological and environmental groups - the Sussex Wildlife Trust, CPRE, English Nature, and bird and butterfly groups. But it was important to get local government on our side. Harold Hall was elected our County Councillor two days before an important meeting at County Hall which would decide the County's policy. He came to be briefed by ABNC, again in the kitchen of Stable Cottage. He must have absorbed the arguments very quickly and put them well; the meeting at County passed a resolution that depending on certain factors, it 'would support the Pink route'. We learnt from Harold that he persuaded the meeting to adopt this instead of the wording that it 'might support the Pink route'.

The Pink route picked up momentum and was widely seen as a sensible compromise. Support came from the District Council (with help from our Councillor, Glynis Hurle-Hobbs) and Walberton and Slindon Parish Councils.

July 1992: A meeting with Kenneth Carlisle

Kenneth Carlisle, who had replaced Christopher Chope as Junior Minister in the Department of Transport, came to see the routes for himself. ABNC took over the conservatory restaurant at the Black Horse pub in Binsted for a meeting with him. Blown-up aerial photos with overlays were put out round the room and we all had lunch, salmon salad. He asked to see the routes 'on the ground'. We set off with me driving, and the Minister and Frank Penfold (author of the Pink route) in the back. In Muddy Lane, I was forced to drive over to one side to avoid ruts, and had a mental image of brambles whipping Mr Carlisle in the face through the back window.

As a result of this meeting (and despite the brambles), he wrote us a letter. It simply said 'ancient woodland of this quality must be left alone'. In January 1993 the Secretary of State announced that he was 'minded to adopt' the Pink route for the Western end, and asked for comments. This was, in effect, the third public consultation.

April 1993: A public meeting at Arundel Town Hall

ABAC (Arundel Bypass Action Committee), the Torton-Hill-based Arundel group, formed in 1990 to press for the Blue route, had refrained from commenting about the Western end of the road (and rejected attempts at co-operation) until the Pink route was endorsed by the Secretary of State. But when it was, the group objected. They came up with what they thought was a better route for the Western end: the 'Green' route through Binsted. (The quotation marks are inescapable. Andrew Lee, Director of the Sussex Wildlife Trust, called it 'anything but green in environmental terms' in a letter to the West Sussex Gazette.) Dr Stenson (a local GP), of ABAC, unveiled the new idea to a packed audience.

ABAC's 'Green' route started as a wide 'corridor' through Binsted, then they selected four different possible routes covering an even wider area. Going east to west, starting near the southernmost point of the Blue route, all four pierced Binsted Park, the beautiful curved field, surrounded by woodland, which once formed the parkland of Binsted House. One version then despoiled the gently undulating fields in the centre of Binsted, once the parish's common land. The other three versions of 'Green' wiped out some of the best, south-western parts of Binsted Woods, like the Orange route. And all were even nearer to the houses of Binsted and its 12th-century church than the Orange route had been.

Many of the arguments for the 'Green' route seemed to be based on misapprehensions. For instance, it was stated that it would 'leave the woodland intact', while in fact three out of its four versions destroyed a lot of the best woodland. Even the one mainly through fields would chop off Little Dane's Wood, Hundred House

Beeches at Binsted Park, near the proposed 'Green route'.

Copse and Barns Copse to the west, and the woodland belts to the south –
fragmentation which would severely damage the Binsted Woods Complex SNCI.   And
that version had an awkward right-angled join with the A27; smoothing it out into a
curve would wipe out Hundred House Copse (a nature reserve leased to the Sussex
Wildlife Trust) and Barn's Copse next to it.

David Tristram and I attended the public meeting.   After the presentation, questions
were asked for.   David Tristram managed a calm question.   Were any of the
environmental organisations (such as supported the Pink route) supporting the 'Green'
route?   The answer was no.

A painful few weeks followed.   ABAC promoted the 'Green' route with a leaflet.
We produced a leaflet pointing out its errors.   More shoeleather was spent on
distributing these round Arundel, Slindon, Binsted and Walberton.   The Department of
Transport decided the 'Green' route should be investigated by its consultants and
compared with the Pink route.

In July 1993 the Pink/Blue route was adopted as the Preferred Route.

Aftermath

This seemed like victory, of a kind.   In 1994 the National Audit Office commended the
Department of Transport for its use of public consultation on the Arundel Bypass.
('There was clear evidence that the public consultation process had a very active and
positive effect on route selection.')   But the next stages (the public advertisement of
'Line Orders', the public inquiry, and then actually building the road) were deferred
again and again.

1995: The torchlight procession

Julia Robson, of South Coast Against Roads (SCAR), had been a constant attender at meetings of ABNC.   She was pleased when the government body called SACTRA (Standing Advisory Committee on Trunk Road Assessment) published a report in 1994 showing that new roads caused more traffic, more congestion and also more development, and that the economic benefits were doubtful.   I can remember Julia saying at a meeting 'development follows roads like spots follow chocolate'.   She saw clearly that the Arundel Bypass was part of a larger scheme: to have a dual carriageway all along the south coast.   SCAR was campaigning against any new road-building on the south coast, in particular against major new bypass schemes at Worthing and

Julia Robson's poster for the torchlit procession to the Madonna Pond in January 1995, to demonstrate against all new road-building on the south coast.

Hastings, as well as Arundel.   The Worthing/Lancing scheme (partly in the suburbs, demolishing 112 houses, and partly on the Downs, including a tunnel) was in fact cancelled in 1996, and the Hastings bypass was cancelled in 2001.

In January 1995 Julia and SCAR members organised a torchlit procession to the Madonna Pond in Binsted.   Parking (ironically) had to be provided, with landrovers at the ready to rescue anyone who got stuck in the mud.   After the torchlit march we gathered round the pond, our flaming torches reflected in the water; speeches were made and poems were read.   A small group sang an eighteenth-century American song about the biblical lily, which toils not, neither does it spin: *'Peaceful and lowly in their native soil/ They neither know to spin nor care to toil,/ Yet in confess'd magnificence deride/ Our mean attire and impotence of pride.'*

A tailpiece to this meeting: when ABNC first formed, Julia was almost the only member who argued against any new road-building.   (Another was Frank Adsett, of Friends of the Earth.)   Julia took her own life in 1999.   But more and more people are coming round to her point of view.   In 1997 I conducted a postal poll of ABNC members on the question of whether or not there should be a new bypass.   The result of the postal vote was a half-and-half split among members of ABNC who replied.

2002: What now?

A struggle is going on at present between County Councils along the south coast, who want bypasses to encourage economic development, and the government, who don't want to spend millions on controversial road schemes unless they have to. The current 'South Coast Multi-Modal Study' (SOCOMMS) has just published its findings, advising the government that the Arundel bypass (and road-building at all the other 'bottlenecks' between Havant and Polegate) should go ahead, along with a package of worthy measures to discourage traffic growth. The study seems to have ignored SACTRA's conclusion in 1994 that new roads themselves cause traffic growth. It has also ignored SACTRA's concern about 'piecemeal improvement', where a series of local bypasses creates a corridor of national significance.

A new factor has entered the scene: the proposed South Downs National Park. The 'Green' route was rejected by the Highways Department's consultants in 1993. But the current deliberations about the National Park may resurrect it. Tortington Common, which would be crossed by the Pink/Blue route, has been included within the draft boundary for the Park. New roads are not allowed in National Parks unless there is no alternative, so if the government decides the Bypass should go ahead, the Department of Transport would have to look at alternatives to the Pink/Blue route. At present, the draft boundary includes most of Binsted Woods but not the rest of Binsted, so the only place to look outside the National Park would be in the fields and copses of Binsted, at something like a version of the 'Green' route.

The 'Green' route is far more damaging than the Pink/Blue route. An attempt to resurrect it would be very controversial, and thus not to the taste of the party in Arundel and the County Council who want a bypass as quickly as possible. But delay may be inevitable. A situation might be created like the one at Okehampton, where, after years of controversy, a special Parliamentary Order had to be passed to enable the A30 dual carriageway Bypass to be built inside Dartmoor National Park. SOCOMMS' linking of all the 'bottlenecks' may also cause delay. It makes little sense to unknot Arundel, only for the increased traffic to meet a worse snarl-up at Worthing.

A long delay would give time for other solutions to be tried: 'improvements' to the present bypass (which could range from minimal to radical); a decision to shift heavy traffic from the A27, near the sensitive Downs, to the A259 further south (especially if developers build the Bognor bypass); even a moratorium on major road-building and investment in public transport. But the British talent for muddling through weighs against any of these. The ghosts of old road schemes, threatening reincarnation, may continue to haunt Binsted for a long time to come.

Chapter 9   Myths and mysteries

Binsted Pond

It is an old Binsted myth that Binsted Pond (known as the Madonna Pond) is
bottomless.   Sue Elphick remembers being told the pond was bottomless when she and
Tony were buying Kent's Cottage, nearby, in 1989.   John Heathcote, Parish Clerk of
Walberton Parish Council until recently, took part in clearing work on the pond with
West Sussex County Council in about 1994.   He says: 'I was expecting a flat or
rounded hard bottom to the pond, because that is what I have found with other ponds I
had dug out before (and since).   We went happily in with a large digger.   The depth of
silt/sludge was much greater than anticipated, and we never got to the bottom of it, for
fear of losing the machine, which was touch and go.

'If we had thought about it a bit more, it is logical that the pond is like the gully on
the other side of the track, and that when the culvert and road were constructed, the
resulting pond was V-shaped rather than U-shaped.   I don't think the depth is
enormous, but equivalent to the gully on the south side, or similar.'

Bill Pethers comments that in the 1980s police frogmen recovered a safe and other
items from the pond and there was no mention of its being bottomless.

The Madonna statue

Other legends have grown up around this atmospheric grove with its dark pond, fallen
trees, and shrine to Our Lady.   Some of these, and other items of Binsted folklore, are
summed up in an article in the Chichester Observer, 13 June 1980, headed 'No Voodoo
in Binsted Woods'.

The Madonna shrine in 2001.

*Suggestions of black magic rituals bound up
with legends of drowned children and
haunted woods have been discounted.*

*Speculation in the remote and straggling
village of Binsted and nearby Walberton
mounted with reports of a shrine to the
Virgin Mary being destroyed and replaced by
a cross and feathers - apparently a possible
symbol of a voodoo brand of black magic.
But the rumours have been described as
'absolute rubbish' by the woman who erected
the shrine 34 years ago, Mrs E. Wishart of
Marsh Farm, Binsted.   She says the
destruction of the shrine - featured in the
Book of Shrines - is just vandalism.   She has*

replaced the damaged life-size figure - a monument to the Virgin Mary in memory of her dead mother - with a tiny replica of the Madonna surrounded by fluffy grasses and artificial flowers in front of a white-painted wooden cross.

Encased in a wooden shelter covered with wire netting and stacked round with barbed wire, the new shrine stands on the old plinth - a tree-trunk painted silver, gold, green and blue with the words Maria Regina Salve Jesus. A fifth word is now indecipherable. It could be that the fluffy grasses decorating the present shrine have been mistaken for feathers and verbal reports of 'a cross and feathers' have been given a significance they do not deserve. But legends of mystery and magic are not new to the eerie and isolated woodland glade where the figure stood overlooking the murky pool in which two children are said to have drowned many years ago.

Local historians say the pool was built as an ornamental lake in the grounds of a manor house which was burnt down before World War II. Mr Dick Coen, of Arundel's Tourist Information Office, said he understood several statues, some stone and some wooden, had been erected there in turn. As for the glade's sinister associations he said: 'It is no more than a persistent rumour. But a lot of people swear blind that when they pass it with their dogs, the dogs start crying and growling. Even those riding by on a horse have a job to get their horses to go on.'

This article contains many errors. Dates given imply the statue was put up in 1946; in fact it was 1952 or 3. The pond was originally one of three fishponds, rather than an 'ornamental lake'. The house was not 'burnt down before World War Two'; though it was no longer lived in, Margaret Pethers was still trying to keep it clean in 1943 or 4; still fairly intact, it was painted by Ralph Ellis in 1946, and much of its ruins remained until recently.

The original, life-size statue (brought back from Italy, where it had been blessed by the Pope) had no 'shelter'. It was painted, with blue robes, but the paint began to peel and a wooden shelter or 'howdah' was put over it. This was smashed up and the statue painted red by vandals. John North recalls being asked by Mrs Wishart to make a shelter for the new, smaller statue out of a birdcage; he thought this impracticable. A new base was made by a Mr Bridges from Arundel. Mr Prosser put a Chubb moneybox in a tree – it was opened within 24 hours; Pat Davy put in another moneybox at some time, equally short-lived. The 'painted plinth' and barbed wire mentioned in the article are long gone. The shrine is now made solidly of brick, with an iron grille to protect the statue. The current brick surround dates from within the last 15 years. The statue itself is a plaster replica.

In spite of the loss of some woodland to the south, on the site of Binsted House (at present a building site), the grove retains its atmosphere and stories will no doubt continue to be told.

Binsted ghosts

When I first put a note in the West Sussex Gazette asking for memories of Binsted, in 2000, Eric Phillips of Felpham sent me the following account.

Whilst driving on the track that runs NE towards Arundel Road, near Goose Green and Meadow Lodge, in about 1980, we were passing over the bridge when I observed a strange character smoking a clay pipe sitting on the low stone bridge wall (the containing walls are now gone because of heavy traffic coming from Arundel and Wishart's farm). His clothes struck me as very strange and old, perhaps over a hundred years. As I passed I looked straight at him and I pulled the car up only 20 feet on to have another look, but lo and behold when I got out in approx. five seconds there was no-one there at all and there was nowhere this person could have gone in such a short time and it has been on my mind ever since.

I returned to the spot recently and found the low wall had gone and the area looked overgrown after the passage of twenty years. I spoke to a young lady who was passing through and lived nearby and I recounted my experience and she seemed rather concerned and mentioned that I could have talked to an older man about it but he had passed on. My wife who was with me in the first instance as we went over the bridge told me she saw nothing on her side of the car, but I saw what I saw and this account now I have put it on paper has in a small way given me some sort of relief.

Eric Phillips' drawing of a ghost seen by him near Meadow Lodge.

Binsted Pond (Madonna Pond).

Ernest Wishart used to say that the Madonna Pond was haunted by a coach and horses which had ridden into it and never come out. The ruins of Binsted House were said to be haunted by a man in a top hat. Bill Pethers remembers an incident from about 1943 or 4 when he was a small child:

'Mother used to go up to the old house and try to keep the place clean. It was a time warp, you would walk through the door and you were back in the 1800s, and nothing had been touched. It was a labour of love, because the old place was falling down, that's the reason why it was abandoned. There was a huge circular box hedge in the centre of the old front garden, not very high, with a gravel path, so you could drive in the main gate in your horse and carriage and drive round and back out again. I remember seeing the old kitchen with stone floors, and the bedrooms virtually as they had been left. One day, I think I was outside playing, and she suddenly rushed out and scooped me up and ran all the way down the road. There was something in there she had to get away from. It was a funny old house, very still, very quiet, and you could be there on a summer's day and feel the hair on the back of your neck stand up. But I must admit I have never seen a ghost in my life.'

When asked who he thought Binsted House was haunted by, he replied 'all my ancestors'! But he has his suspicions that the ghost Mr Phillips saw might have been the real form of his father, Henry Pethers.

Flying saucers and UFOs

Helen Whitlock, of Goose Green, Binsted, had a strange experience in 1995.

It was in the early hours of Saturday morning of July 1st, 1995.   To be exact, the time was 2.45 a.m. - I always go to bed in the early hours so hence the time.   It was a very hot humid night and very still.   I went out into the back garden with the dogs to let them have their last sniff before going to bed.   I gazed up at the sky and I had not seen so many stars for a long time.   It was while I was admiring these that suddenly this object glided over the middle of our roof, it was about forty foot high above me.   It was quite long and shaped like a cigar with rounded ends, with a ring of thick white mist round the middle of it, and from either side at the back of it were four long straight lines of very bright lights, two outer green ones and two inner red ones.   There was no noise at all coming from this object, completely silent, it did not disturb the dogs or horses in any way.   I watched it go over our paddocks very slowly towards Tortington then suddenly it put on a terrific spurt and just vanished into thin air as they say. I waited for a while in case it came back but no, so I went up to bed full of wonder, vowing to myself that I would not mention this to my family or to anyone else in case they thought that I was making it up or worse still going round the bend.

I would have kept to that had it not been for the events of the following morning. To the south side of our house we have a large natural pond, to reach this pond you have to climb down a steep bank which is covered in tall reeds. The whole of the pond and banks are completely enclosed with a post and rail fence so it is nearly impossible for anything large to get in there. After breakfast Robin, my husband, went down to the pond to feed the moorhens who live on our pond all the year round. After a short while he called out to me 'come and look at this'. When I got to the pond to my amazement there was a vast area of completely flattened reeds in a large circle as though something really heavy had been lying there. It was perfectly all right the night before, we were both mystified, so then I decided to tell him what had taken place in the early hours of the morning.

Maybe we will never know what really happened in those early hours, but I must admit each time I go into the garden at night I always do a Patrick Moore and look at 'the sky at night', just in case.

The book *Fields of Mystery: The Crop Circle Phenomenon in Sussex*, by Andy Thomas (S.B. Publications, 1996) described this happening and said there were no traces of anyone having broken into the area, and there was no apparent physical damage to the plants. Although the shape of the 'splurge' was fairly indiscernible, the rushes appeared to be 'laid and swirled in much the same way one would expect in a more usual event'. As far as he knew, this was the first instance in England of a 'formation' having been reported in rushes.

Brendon Staker had a similar experience as a child.

One August evening about 1975, my mother, brother, cousin and I went blackberry picking on Binsted Brooks below Hoe Lane. It was just starting to get dark, so we decided to go home. We went across Footpath Brook, over the bridge and on to Langmead's Brooks towards the Cattle Crossing. We had just got over the Cattle Crossing on the railway line when we all stopped and looked in the sky and this object hovered above at a maximum height of 100 feet. It stayed there for about two minutes and it had a saucer shape to it with rows of lights going round it, then moved off into a south-westerly direction and then landed in one of Mr Langmead's fields called Six Acres. By then we were frightened and rushed home to ask my father if he had seen anything but he was indoors. My father said that a German plane was shot down and crashed in that field and to this day I still do not understand what it was!!!

Knacker's Hole

Luke Wishart writes that the 'Knacker Hole' in Burgess's Field, south of Goose Green, is 'nothing to do with planes or bombs. This was a mythical hole, like the one at Lyminster which houses a dragon. Said to be the home of dragons, and bottomless. Being of a scientific frame of mind, I arranged to place our irrigation pump into it to test the water capacity. The pump ran dry in just over 10 hours, and we could see the bottom. It filled up rapidly as soon as we stopped pumping. We didn't find any dragons – but to keep the myth going, they may have escaped overnight.'

Ghosts   E.T.

On winter's slopes a grey mist scarf
Twists and drapes when you cross the rife
Into Binsted.   Past the thickening rough
Golfers quack now where deer once froze,
But something in the valley hears
Your progress.   The mist girl twirls and bows.

At the top of the hill the Black Horse rears
Its grotesque grin; the old inn-sign
No longer seen, plain black on green,
Nor those smoked, spilling crowds of war
With beer in buckets by the door.
Some didn't come back.   They dipped for
    more.

Round the next bend, you may scare a cloud
Of myths and secrets, starved for words:
They twitter of gardens in the woods,
Wandering loves, unofficial lives
Forgiven, or mossed into graves,
Lost after years like the whitewashed tales

Briefly alight on the church's walls.
Soldiers, Saviour, lovers, spies,
Their soft ghosts press on one who drives
Too quickly round the further curves
Of our lazy lane, towards the Park
Where a dark pool holds trees as dark.

Now they crowd thicker; turkeys, geese,
Children at pasture, browsing cows,
Exploring aliens; devotees
Of Halloween fires; and all who pray
To a Madonna they found one day
At a shrine in the woods, by a pond, with
    flowers.

The creaking, carol-singing trunks
Bend to our journey; full of work
Once, shadows now, they point
Back to the church, where a painting still
Challenges with its blinded gaze:
Margaret or Mary?   Or Ambrose?

Six saints: a Bishop, a Saxon queen,
Another saved from a dragon's womb,
A Magdalene, with unctuous hair,
Or the Queen of Heaven.   Peter, too,
Mentioned somewhere.   The cock that crew
Points north-east on the shingled spire.

Voices like feathers flock the air;
Sometimes they touch you.   Nothing to fear,
The mist of breath on the quiet we've kept,
Rooks pass, not cars, on a road unbuilt -
Something to warm us, something rare,
The stuff of our Millennium quilt.

Painting of Binsted House by Charlotte Read.

The Read family with a fallen oak in Binsted Park.

Bibliography

1. Historical background

Anderson, M.D., *The Imagery of British Churches*, London, John Murray (1955).

Bell, Mrs Arthur, *The Saints in Christian Art*, London, Bell and Sons (1902).

Coward, B., *The Stuart Age: England 1603-1714*, London, Longman (1994).

Evans, E.J., *The Forging of the Modern State:Early Industrial Britain 1783-1870*, London, Longman (1998).

Gillingham, J. and Griffiths, R.A., *Medieval Britain*, Oxford, Oxford University Press (1984).

Needham, A., *How to Study an Old Church*, London, Batsford (1948).

Parsons, G., *Religion in Victorian England: Traditions*, Manchester, Manchester University Press (1988).

Platt, C., *The Parish Churches of Medieval England*, London, Secker & Warburg (1981).

Platt, C., *King Death: The Black Death and its aftermath in late-medieval England*, London, UCL Press (1997).

Rodwell, W. & Bentley, J., *Our Christian Heritage*, London, Guild Publishing (1984).

Schama, S., *A History of Britain, At the Edge of the World? 3000BC-AD1603*, London, BBC Worldwide (2000).

Smith, A.G.R., *The Emergence of a Nation State: The Commonwealth of England 1529-1660*, London, Longman (1997).

Smith, E., Cook, O. and Hutton, G., *English Parish Churches*, London, Thames & Hudson (1976).

2. Local history

The Victoria History of the County of Sussex, Volume V, Part 1, Arundel Rape (South-Western Part), including Arundel (Oxford University Press, 1997), section on Binsted by Heather M. Warne.   Many of the journal articles and documents referred to in its copious footnotes can be viewed at the West Sussex Records Office in Chichester.

3. Archaeology

Ainsworth, C., 'A tile and pottery kiln at Binsted, Sussex', *Mediaeval Archaeology*, Vol. XI 316-17 (1967).

Barton, K.J., *Mediaeval Sussex Pottery* (London and Chichester, Phillimore, 1979).

Bradley, R., 'A field survey of the Chichester Entrenchments', in B.W. Cunliffe, *Excavations At Fishbourne*, Vol. 1, Comm. Soc. Antiq. Vol. 26 (1971).

Holmes, J., 'The Chichester Dykes', *Sussex Archaeological Collections*, Vol. 106, 63-72 (1968).

Murray, K.M.E., 'The Chichester earthworks', *Sussex Archaeological Collections*, Vol. 94, 139-43 (1956).

4. General

Grove, Valerie, *Laurie Lee: the Well-loved Stranger*, London, Viking/Penguin (1999).

Pevsner, Nikolaus, and Ian Nairn, *The Buildings of England: Sussex* (1965).

Thomas, Andy, *Fields of Mystery: The Crop Circle Phenomenon in Sussex* (S.B. Publications, 1996).